THE GUINNESS BOOK OF

BRITAIN

Records, Facts and Feats

Researched and Edited by

JAMES TINDALL

English
Tourist Board

Northern Ireland
Tourist Board

BWRDD CROESO CYMRU
WALES TOURIST BOARD

STB

SCOTTISH
TOURIST
BOARD

GUINNESS PUBLISHING

In-house Editor: Paola Simoneschi
Design and Layout: Kathy Aldridge
Cover Design: David Roberts

Typeset in Great Britain by Ace Filmsetting Ltd, Frome, Somerset
Printed and bound in Great Britain by Butler & Tanner Ltd, Frome

A catalogue record for this book is available from the British Library

ISBN 0-85112-587-5

Contents

Introduction

Welcome to a guide book with a difference. *The Guinness Book of Britain* is a unique overview of Great Britain and Northern Ireland – a celebration of the best of Britain in both the natural and the man-made world.

It contains information on around 500 British superlatives including, as appropriate, the highest, tallest, largest, smallest, oldest and even most-visited, ranging from mountains and lakes through castles and cathedrals to inns and office blocks.

The natural beauty of the many diverse parts of Britain includes tranquil Lough Neagh, the dramatic cliffs and sea stacks of the northern Scottish coast, brooding Snowdonia and the breathtaking Dorset coast.

Man-made superlatives range from the finest remains of Stone- and Iron-Age man, such as Stonehenge and Skara Brae, to the incredible construction achievements of the late 20th century, including Canary Wharf and the Eurotunnel. Over the centuries each group of master builders has left its own superlatives as enduring evidence of its prowess.

The Romans gave us thousands of structures, the dramatic remains of which we are still in awe of nearly 2000 years later. These include Fishbourne Palace, the baths at Bath and Hadrian's Wall.

The veil that fell across Britain during the Dark Ages is occasionally parted, particularly in the religious centres of Iona and Lindisfarne.

Norman times onwards are well-represented, particularly by the spectacular castles and cathedrals and, in more peaceful times, great houses and parks.

Britain was the cradle of the Industrial Revolution, something anyone visiting Ironbridge will never forget, while the Victorian engineers were probably the greatest and most adventurous builders since the Romans. Their railways, bridges and civic buildings are simply magnificent.

The 20th century has seen the application of new technologies to old problems and the rise in importance of roads and airports. An example of the enduring visible images of the second half of the 20th century are the immense and beautiful suspension bridges crossing Britain's widest estuaries.

What might surprise readers of this book is the number of these British superlatives that are also world or European superlatives. It is also full of odd facts. For example, did you realise that there are more beds available for visitors in Blackpool than there are in the whole of Portugal? Or that Harry Ramsden's Fish and Chip Shop fries 213 tons of fish a year to feed a million customers?

This celebration of the best of Britain unfolds as we approach the end of the 20th century. It is intended to be a guide for lovers of Britain, as well as a fact-filled reference book and an argument-solver.

Now that the 'work' is done, I am going to select my own favourite ten superlatives. I offer my apologies to the others I have researched and listed in this book but these are just my personal 'bests', the things I like most about Britain [listed in no particular order]:

- **Wast Water in Cumbria**
- **Lulworth Cove in the West Country**
- **The Giant's Causeway in Northern Ireland**
- **Hadrian's Wall in Northumbria**
- **Caerphilly Castle in South Wales**
- **Salisbury Cathedral in the West Country**
- **The Palace Pier at Brighton in the South East**
- **Charlotte Square in Edinburgh**
- **The Humber Bridge in Yorkshire and Humberside**
- **The Dove Inn in Hammersmith, west London**

The four National Tourist Boards have been invaluable in the creation of this book. They supplied their own suggestions for superlatives and read through the draft manuscript to check my various eccentricities, as did the Regional Tourist Boards in England, who brought a great deal of local knowledge to bear. The Tourist Boards also drew on their information resources to provide the latest audited visitor numbers and, through the excellent Britain in View photo library, provided most of the splendid photographs.

This is the first edition of *The Guinness Book of Britain*, I hope that you enjoy it and find it useful and thought-provoking. It is not exhaustive so, if you feel that something dramatic has been omitted, please write to me via Guinness Publishing and I will check your suggestion. If you are right, it will be included in the next edition.

I must thank a few people for bringing about this project: Donald McFarlan of Guinness Publishing and Richard Dorsett and Michael Dewing of the English Tourist Board for believing that we could do it, and Jill, Trouble and Strife, for ensuring that we did.

James Tindall, 1993

THE GUINNESS BOOK OF

BRITAIN

Records, Facts and Feats

The 'Druid's Altar', Islandmagee, N. Ireland.

The South West

Moors and Historic Towns, Caves and a Unique Theatre

Devon, Cornwall and the Isles of Scilly form the southwestern extremity of the island of Britain and present a distinctive landscape of moors, granite tors, cliffs and sheltered estuaries. The moorlands include two National Parks, the western part of Exmoor and the whole of Dartmoor and Bodmin Moor.

The estuaries in this region are rias, i.e. flooded river valleys. Some, such as Plymouth Sound, are associated with major events in British naval history whilst others, such as romantic Helford River, are havens for modern yachtsmen.

Nowadays, much of the South West has tourism as its prime industry but the landscape is dotted with evidence of other, older occupations. Some have all but disappeared – for example, the tin mines that provided prosperity from Roman times onwards – but others, like the great slate quarry at Delabole, are still active.

There are also examples of ancient man's existence, ingenuity and inventiveness in the area, from 40 000 years ago at Kent's Cavern to the 20th century at the remarkable Minack Theatre.

Moorlands (and literature)

The three major moorlands in the region each have their own individual characteristics and their own distinctive, world-famous literary associations.

Exmoor

Exmoor is the smallest National Park in England. Covering 686 km² (265 sq. miles), it was founded in 1954 and straddles the boundary of Devon and Somerset. The moor is a high-level plateau averaging 425 m (1400 ft), with its highest point at Dunkery Beacon, 517 m (1705 ft). Its northern boundary runs along the coast producing some spectacular clifflines. For most people, however, Exmoor will always be Doone country, the setting for R.D. Blackmore's romantic classic, *Lorna Doone*.

Bodmin Moor

Bodmin Moor in Cornwall is a granite moorland approximately 200 km² (80 sq. miles) in area, similar to Dartmoor but at a lower level. Its highest point is a tor called Brown Willy, 417 m (1375 ft). There is much evidence of ancient man's existence in the area and Dozmary Pool is often referred to as the last resting place of King Arthur's legendary sword, Excalibur. A coaching inn at the centre of the moor was the setting for Daphne du Maurier's world-renown novel, *Jamaica Inn*.

Dartmoor

Dartmoor was created a National Park in 1951 and covers 945 km² (365 sq. miles) of Devon. It is a rolling landscape of uplands, bogs and broad river valleys, with an average elevation of 364 m (1200 ft), topped by isolated granite tors, the two highest of which are High Willays at 618 m (2038 ft) and Yes Tor at 616 m (2030 ft). At its centre is the famous Dartmoor Prison, but its greatest 'claim to fame' worldwide is undoubtedly as the location for Arthur Conan Doyle's classic Sherlock Holmes story, *The Hound of the Baskervilles*.

Left: The world-famous Jamaica Inn.

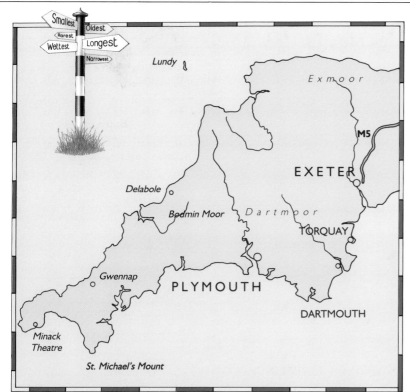

Islands

Lundy Island

Lundy Island is located 19 km (12 miles) NNW of Devon's Hartland Point. It is roughly 5 km (3 miles) long by 1 km (⅝ mile) wide, with cliffs rising straight out of the sea to heights of over 90 m (300 ft) and a highest point of 142 m (466 ft).

It is a wildlife paradise, the main island being home to ponies, deer and rabbits whilst small Rat Island is, unsurprisingly, famous as the home of wild black rats. But Lundy is most famous for its birdlife, the high cliffs harbour colonies of hundreds of species of birds that are rare or non-existent on the mainland, including falcons, cormorants, oyster-catchers and, above all, puffins. The puffin colon-

Below: Dartmoor viewed south from Haytor.

ies of Lundy have been famous for centuries and the island's name is thought to derive from Scandinavia and means, literally, Puffin Island.

Below: Lundy – 'Puffin Island'.

St. Michael's Mount

St. Michael's Mount is in Mount's Bay close to Penzance. It is not truly an island as a causeway connects it to the Cornish mainland at low tide. It is a wooded granite outcrop of 8.5 ha (21 acres) topped by a romantic 14th-century castle and is one of the most photographed spots in Britain.

The Scilly Isles

The Scilly Isles are a cluster of about 300 granite islands and islets 45 km (28 miles) southwest of Lands End. They are the last outcropping of the Cornish granite massifs and are both the most westerly and the most southerly points in England.

The islands are virtually unspoilt and have a very mild climate. They are famous for their early spring flowers and one of the islands, Tresco, has extensive sub-tropical gardens featuring plants brought to the Scillies from all over the world.

Left: Doone country – Exmoor, Devon.

Exeter

Exeter's origins appear to have been in the Iron Age. The Romans established a walled settlement there, the Saxons founded a number of churches and, for a time, held out against a siege mounted by William the Conqueror. Once they had overcome the resistance, the Normans built their castle and cathedral, as was their custom, and Exeter became the most important town in the South West.

Exeter Cathedral

The present Exeter Cathedral dates from 1275 and its most impressive feature is its spectacular ceiling vaulting – stretching more than 90 m (300 ft) through both the nave and the choir, it is the longest stretch of Gothic vaulting in Britain.

Guildhall

Exeter's Guildhall was built in 1468, although the present frontage dates from 1592. It is still used by Exeter City Council and is the oldest municipal building in England still in continuous use.

Ship Canal

To Exeter also goes the honour of having the oldest ship canal in Britain. During the Middle Ages, Exeter was a busy port with ships sailing up the river Exe to the city's quays. The city fathers quarrelled with the owner of the lands to the south of the city, Isabella de Fortibus, Countess of Devon, and she retaliated by building a weir across the Exe. With no access to the sea, Exeter's fortunes suffered and the citizens decided that they would have to dig their way out of the problem. The first phase of the canal linked the city with the Exe below the weir and was opened in 1566. The stretch included the first lock gates to be erected in Britain.

Plymouth

Plymouth is one of the greatest naval centres in Britain. This is primarily because of the existence of Plymouth Sound, a great natural anchorage formed where a number of rivers, including the Tamar and the Plym, drain into the sea. Plymouth Sound covers an area of 1820

Below: Tresco's breathtaking sub-tropical gardens.

Clifftop Theatre

Porthcurno is on the Cornish coast between Penzance and Land's End. Miss Rowena Cade, an actress, lived in an isolated house overlooking the rugged 60 m (200 ft) high granite cliffs. They dropped down to the sea in a series of steps and Miss Cade conceived the idea of creating a Grecian amphitheatre on the cliffside. Work began in 1932 and was undertaken almost entirely by herself and her gardener. Over the decades, Miss Cade continued to expand her dream, creating a stage surface, seating and dressing rooms.

The result of her work is an open-air theatre in the most spectacular setting, with the ocean and Cornwall's incomparable cliff scenery as the backdrop to summer evenings of Shakespeare and other performances. The Minack Theatre is unique and is a fitting memorial to a remarkable lady.

ha (4500 acres) and is easily defensible from surrounding headlands and fortified islands.

In 1439, Plymouth was the first town in England to be incorporated by Act of Parliament rather than through the monarch.

Above: The plaque commemorating the departure of the Pilgrim Fathers.

The town and its famous waterside promenade, the Hoe, established their place in the history books in 1588, when Sir Francis Drake, on being informed of the approach of the feared enemy fleet, the Spanish Armada, insisted on completing his game of bowls before setting sail to defeat it. Whether this was the cool and controlled attitude of an English gentleman, or merely the calculations of the sailor who knew that the tide was not right to sail on and he could finish his game, we will never know.

Plymouth is also famous as the point of departure of the Pilgrim Fathers in 1620. They left from Mayflower Steps to form their colonies in the New World.

Royal Dockyard

Plymouth became a Royal Dockyard in 1690, a few years after Charles II's massive 152-gun fortress, the Citadel, had been built alongside the Hoe. It has been a major base for the Royal Navy ever since.

Dartmouth

Another part of the region with strong Royal Navy associations is Dartmouth. The imposing buildings of the Britannia Royal Naval College were opened in 1905 and dominate the town.

Dartmouth Castle, protecting the town and located just downstream from it, was built between 1481 and 1495 and was the first castle in Britain designed specifically for artillery, with gun ports rather than arrow slits built into the walls.

Mines and Quarries

Cornwall is littered with mineral works, and the image most associated with the county is probably that of a derelict tin mine's engine house and chimney framed on a clifftop against the sea. There are two examples of Cornwall's mining and quarrying past that are particularly worthy of note . . .

Delabole

The Delabole Slate Quarry is just inland from Tintagel and is still a working

Below: Tin mine engine houses, Redruth.

quarry. Its famous blue-grey slates were first excavated in the 15th century, while the quarry itself was started in 1570 and, by 1602, it was already referred to as 'a notable hole'. Today, the 'notable hole' is the largest quarry in Britain, having a circumference of 2.6 km (1.6 miles) and a depth of 150 m (500 ft).

Gwennap

The Gwennap Pit is just east of Redruth and is the site of disused mine works. The land surface sank through weakening caused by the workings and formed a 'natural' amphitheatre. Exactly when the collapse happened is not clear but,

in 1743, a crowd recorded as hundreds or thousands gathered in the amphitheatre to hear John Wesley preach Methodism as the way forward for the miners. The sides of Gwennap Pit were cut into terraces of seating in 1806, and since 1807, it has been the location for an annual May Day service to celebrate Wesley's famous sermon.

Ancient man

The South West holds many remains of Stone-Age man, including burial tombs and circles, but one simple cave is the most important.

Above: Dartmouth Castle – the first British castle designed specifically for artillery.

Kent's Cavern, near Torquay, was known in the 16th century but scientific investigations of the cave's contents and compacted floor-covering only began in 1825. What has been revealed is that the cave was used as a shelter by man around 40 000 years ago. Also, animal remains show that early man shared the shelter of the cave. Remains that have been found include those of mammoths, woolly rhinoceros, bison and giant deer.

The West Country Fringes

Spectacular Scenery and Historic Sites

This region covers the counties of Avon, Somerset and most of Dorset and includes some superb scenery ranging from the Dorset coast to the Mendip Hills and the eastern part of Exmoor.

Like neighbouring Wiltshire, the area is home to ancient relics, including Maiden Castle, the greatest Iron-Age fortress in Europe, and the Cerne Giant. Glastonbury and its Tor are renowned for their mystical associations, while the Roman remains in the city of Bath are world-famous, as are its elegant Georgian terraces and crescents.

The region has a mighty city in Bristol and a tiny one in Wells, the smallest cathedral city in England. Both have distinctive attractions.

The area is also the site of the last battle on English soil and houses the biggest and oldest swannery in England.

The Classic Cove

The coastline of Dorset is regarded as being amongst the most attractive in Britain, with many spectacular features.

Lulworth Cove

Geography textbooks explain that a cove is formed when the rock strata runs parallel to the coastline with first a layer of hard, resistant rock, then a layer of softer, more erodable rock and finally another layer of hard rock. The sea eventually cuts through the first layer in one small place, rapidly erodes the second layer but is again halted by the third layer, forming a circular bay with a narrow, steep entrance to the sea and cliffs behind. Throw the textbooks away. Go and stand on the cliffs above Lulworth Cove and you will *instantly* understand what the geographers are trying to communicate. Lulworth is the classic textbook cove. Going west along the coast you will reach Durdle Door, a classic sea arch, Portland Bill and Chesil Beach.

Below: Lulworth Cove – the textbook classic.

Chesil Beach

Chesil Beach is a 16 km (10 mile) long sea bar (the longest in Europe), linking the coast near Abbotsbury with Portland. Its width varies from 180 m (600 ft) to 900 m (3000 ft) and it is composed entirely of pebbles and shingle which progressively increase in size from west to east. It is the purity of the size grading of its constituent stones that make Chesil Beach unique in Europe. The beach encloses a lagoon called the Fleet on its landward side.

The Mendips

The Mendip Hills are made of limestone and show all of the classic features of a limestone landscape with gorges and caves. Cheddar Gorge is the largest gorge in Britain and at its deepest point its floor is 150 m (500 ft) below the surrounding land surface.

Cheddar Gorge also contains two spectacular cave systems, Cox's and Gough's. Both systems were first discovered in the 19th century and are still being explored, although evidence has emerged that the caves provided shelter for humans more than 10 000 years ago.

Dorchester

The Dorchester area appears to have been a very important one for Stone-age man. Within 24 km (15 miles) of the town there are 12 neolithic hill forts and the greatest of these, Maiden Castle, is only 3 km (2 miles) southwest of Dorchester.

Maiden Castle

Maiden Castle was first occupied around 2000BC and there is clear evidence of both a stone-age settlement and an iron-age fort.

By the time of the Roman invasion, the Castle was a huge and very complex structure which served as the headquarters of the Durotriges tribe. Its succession of huge mounds and ditches,

with complicated maze-like entrances through the defences, was undoubtedly awe-inspiring as the structure spreads over 50 ha (124 acres) of the hilltop. It took the organisation and experience of battle-tested Roman legions to break through the barriers, in AD44, and conquer the defenders of Maiden Castle. It is the largest hill fort in Europe.

Closer to the centre of Dorchester are the Maumbury Rings. They originally formed a ritual stone circle erected in the Stone Age.

When the Romans settled in Dorchester, they converted the circle into an amphitheatre capable of holding audiences of more than 10 000 watching gladiatorial combat. In medieval times, the amphitheatre was used as a site for jousting, bear-baiting and cockfighting and, in the 17th and 18th centuries, it was the place for public executions,

Above: Maiden Castle, Dorset.

events that attracted audiences as large as the Roman combats.

Justice

Justice in Dorchester was often imposed severely. In 1685, it was the site of Judge Jefferies' Bloody Assize following the Duke of Monmouth's Rebellion and, in 1834, the Tolpuddle

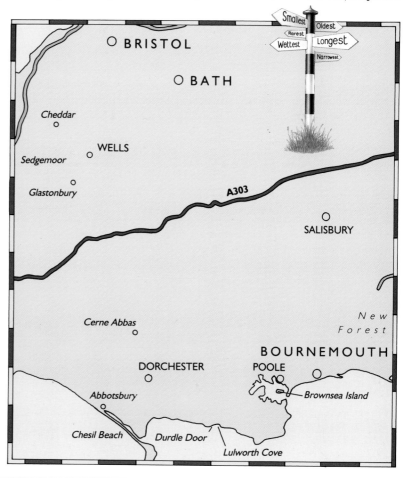

Martyrs were tried at Dorchester and deported to Australia for trying to form an early trade union.

Hardy's Home

On a lighter note, the great novelist Thomas Hardy was born in 1840 and lived in the Dorchester area, dying at Max Gate in Dorchester on 11 January, 1928.

Cerne Giant

North of Dorchester is the village of Cerne Abbas where the hillside overlooking the village is dominated by the Cerne Giant, a huge figure which was probably cut into the hillside around AD190 (although it could have been earlier), and is normally regarded as a figure of Hercules. The rampant and warlike figure is 55 m (180 ft) high, 51 m (167 ft) wide and carries a club 37 m (120 ft) long. It is the largest figure of its type in Britain.

The Last Battle

The last battle to take place on English soil happened on 6 July, 1685, on Sedgemoor, east of the town of Bridgwater. James, Duke of Monmouth, was in rebellion against the King and gathered 3700 men to his side. A royalist force of 2500 troops met and defeated them and the ferocity of the revenge and retribution exacted on Monmouth's men and their sympathisers was appalling. Thousands were rounded up, tried, often by Judge Jefferies, and executed or transported.

Glastonbury

Glastonbury Tor

Glastonbury Tor rises 159 m (522 ft) above the surrounding Somerset Levels. From a distance it looks like a magical and mysterious place, particularly when the Levels are shrouded in mist and the Tor appears to be riding on the top of them.

In earlier centuries, the Tor was undoubtedly an island standing amidst the flooded Levels. Maybe this is part of the reason why there are so many legends linked with Glastonbury.

Christian Visitors

Glastonbury Abbey was a rich and powerful religious centre until the Dissolution. The origin of the religious settlement is said to have been a group of early Christian missionaries from Rome who reached Glastonbury in AD166, making it the oldest religious settlement in Britain.

However, legend has it that Glastonbury had an even earlier Christian visitor. It is reputed that in AD63 Joseph of

Below: The rampant Cerne Giant.

Above: Glastonbury Tor.

Arimathea visited. He was the man whose tomb Christ was buried in, and it is said that Joseph brought with him to Glastonbury the Holy Grail, the chalice used at the Last Supper. He is supposed to have buried the Holy Grail in the side of the Tor at the source of Chalice Well.

Swanning Around

Abbotsbury is a pretty village at the western end of Chesil Beach. The Abbotsbury Swannery is on the Fleet, waters trapped by Chesil Beach, and has a unique collection of mute swans. Founded in the 14th century, it is also the largest swannery in Britain, with 500 swans and many other species of birds.

His staff, so the story goes, was also planted in the ground and grew into the Glastonbury Thorn, which flowered every Christmas.

Arthur's Resting Place?

King Arthur and Queen Guinevere are said to be buried in Glastonbury Tor, having been transported to Avalon on a barge to await the return of Camelot.

Legends or not, these tales undoubtedly add to the 'other worldliness' that is Glastonbury.

Wells

Wells is the smallest cathedral city in England, with a population of less than 9000, and it contains some fascinating buildings . . .

The West Front of the Cathedral is an incredible early-English structure with 297 statues in niches covering its surface.

Left: The Cathedral in Wells, England's smallest cathedral city.

The neighbouring Bishop's Palace was built at the end of the 13th century, although its walls and moat were added in 1340 as a defensive precaution when the then archbishop was in dispute with the townspeople.

Vicar's Close is the oldest inhabited street in western Europe – its buildings date from the 14th century.

Aquae Sulis

The hot mineral springs of the Bath area were known from Iron-age times onwards but it was the arrival of the Romans that made them famous.

The springs produce 1 000 000 litres (250 000 gallons) of water a day at a constant temperature of 48°C (118°F) and, in the 1st century AD, the Romans built bath houses over them and erected a temple to Sul Minerva alongside.

The baths were very elaborate with cold plunge pools and a central hot, shallow swimming pool lined in lead from the Mendips. The centrepiece of the temple was a bronze status of Minerva, the Roman goddess of wisdom and healing. The Roman town around the Baths was called *Aquae Sulis*.

After the Romans left England, the site became derelict and was buried until 1727, when the bronze head of Minerva was uncovered. The location of the Baths was revealed in 1755, although it was some years later that the Great Bath was discovered. The remains form the best-preserved Roman bath-house in Britain and the second greatest Roman remain in the country, after Hadrian's Wall.

Bath had re-emerged as a major spa town before the Roman remains were uncovered, mainly due to the efforts of Richard 'Beau' Nash, who lived from 1674 to 1762. His energy and vision inspired the creators of Georgian Bath, two of the greatest of whom were father and son, John Wood the Elder and Younger. Between them they created Queens Square from 1728, The Circus

Above: Bath Abbey.

from 1754, Royal Crescent from 1769 and the Pump Room from 1796.

Bristol Fashion

Bristol was founded during Anglo-Saxon times but its growth as a major port began in the 12th century and was boosted when trade with the American colonies started.

Brunel's Legacy

The city was shaped by many individuals but one man in particular left an amazing number of lasting memorials to his skills. Isambard Kingdom Brunel, the great engineer, undertook a great deal of work in the Bristol area.

In 1830, he constructed the docks and in 1841 his Great Western Railway reached its western terminus at Temple Meads Station, which he also constructed. His two great ships, SS *Great Western* and SS *Great Britain* were built in Bristol.

Brunel's last design, for the Clifton Suspension Bridge over the Avon, was completed after his death and was opened in 1864.

SS *Great Britain*, which is 98 m (322 ft) long, was the world's first iron-hulled, screw-driven passenger ship and was also the largest ship in the world when it was launched in 1843. It has now been returned to Bristol, is being restored and is on display in the original dry dock where it was built. The dry dock was also built by Brunel.

Religious Centre

Bristol has long been a religious centre for all types of Christian worship – especially the non-conformist. The New Room in Broadmead was the first Methodist Chapel in the world and served as John Wesley's headquarters from 1739.

Opposite: The magnificent Clifton Suspension Bridge – Brunel's last design.

Southern England

Ancient Man, Mighty Oaks . . . and Boy Scouts!

Wiltshire, Hampshire and the Isle of Wight are often thought of as a sort of buffer zone. They are too far from London to be regarded as part of the Home Counties but not far enough away to be part of the West Country.

The truth is that the region includes a wide range of landscapes, ranging from the starkness of Salisbury Plain to the ancient New Forest and the varied coastlines of Hampshire and the Isle of Wight.

Southern England, particularly Wiltshire, held a kind of magical attraction for ancient Man, and the area is littered with his monuments, particularly around Avebury and Stonehenge.

To a lesser extent, a similar attraction continued throughout the Roman occupation, the dark ages and medieval England. Winchester was the capital of England for more than 200 years and Salisbury Cathedral is one of the most attractive and photogenic cathedrals in the country.

Above all, Southern England is renowned for its maritime associations. The Isle of Wight almost looks like a bottle stopper that has been pulled south out of the neck of the bottle that is the Solent and Southampton Water. These waters, with the shelter provided by the isle, the natural harbours, the rare double tides and the ease of fortification on both sides, have been important since Roman times and have been key maritime centres since the Tudor period. Today, they offer pleasure-sailing at Cowes and the Hamble, routes for commercial traffic from Southampton and a home to the Royal Navy at Portsmouth.

Ancient Man and Mystic Monuments

A map of England showing only the remains of Stone- and Bronze-age man would reveal a remarkable concentration on the Wiltshire Downs and Salisbury Plain. Such a concentration can be partially explained by the fact that, 5000 years ago, the chalk downlands with their sparse, short vegetation would have been like islands amongst the densely forested lowlands. What *cannot* be explained is why tens of thousands of men spent hundreds of years erecting vastly complex structures on this region's downlands.

Avebury

Avebury is about 8 km (5 miles) west of Marlborough. Within 3 km (2 miles) of the village are five major ancient constructions – Silbury Hill, West Kennett Long Barrow, Windmill Hill, the Sanctuary, and Avebury itself.

Above: Silbury Hill.

Silbury Hill was constructed about 2700BC. It is a huge artificial mound 40 m (130 ft) high while its base covers an area of 2.2 ha (5.4 acres). It is thought to be the burial mound of a great leader and took more than a generation to raise. There have been a number of excavations to try and uncover the burial tomb but Silbury is so big that it refuses to reveal its secrets. It is the largest artificial mound in Europe.

The West Kennett Long Barrow is a chambered tomb which was constructed c. 2000BC. It was the communal burial place for an important family and was used for around 300 years. The remains of 30 bodies have been discovered in its chambers. Measuring 106 m (350 ft) long, West Kennett is one of the longest barrows in Europe.

Windmill Hill is a series of three concentric earthworks which were constructed c. 2400BC by neolithic farmers, probably as a means of corralling their animals. When first investigated, it was thought to be unique and all early farmers of the Stone Age are still given the name Windmill Hill People.

The Sanctuary is the oldest of the remains in this area, having been constructed c. 2900BC. It consisted of two

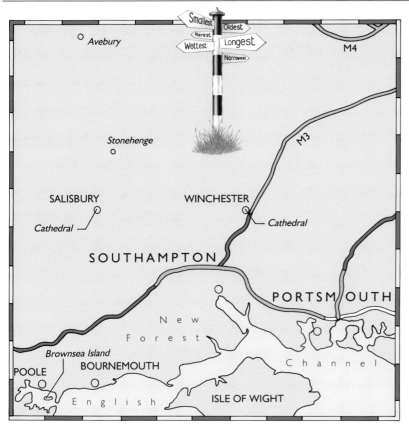

concentric stone circles, the outer one being 12 m (39 ft) in diameter. It is 1.6 km (1 mile) from the main Avebury site and is linked to it by the West Kennett Avenue, a double line of stones.

Avebury itself is very complex and was constructed c. 2600BC. It consisted of four structures: the Northern Inner Circle had a ring of 12 stones surrounded by a second ring of 27 stones; the Southern Inner Circle had one ring of 30 stones with a central Obelisk, and both Inner Circles were surrounded by a great outer Stone Circle made of 98 sarcen blocks. This Stone Circle was in turn surrounded by a 9 m (30 ft) deep ditch with four causeways across it.

The exact purpose of Avebury is unclear but it would appear to have been a religious monument. It was in use for around 500 years but, after 2100BC, it was abandoned when all religious attention became focused on the great

Below: Avebury Stone Circle.

stone circle 24 km (15 miles) to the south, known as Stonehenge.

Stonehenge

The area around Stonehenge obviously held great significance for early Man before the structure was erected. Within 16 km (10 miles) of the site, there are 12 long barrows constructed from around 4000BC onwards.

Stonehenge itself is unique in two ways. Firstly, because it is the only site in the country where the stones were pounded and shaped to fit the structures the builders wanted to create. Secondly, because it shows distinct periods of improvements, re-building and embellishment over a 1700-year period between 2800BC and 1100BC.

Above: World-famous Stonehenge.

The earliest structure was a ditch with an unusual inner mound and a circle of 56 pits, known as Aubrey Holes, which were constructed between 2800BC and 2300BC.

In 2200BC, a stone circle was constructed within the ditch, but the major work commenced in 2100BC when 80 huge sarcen stones, some weighing up to 50 tons, were hauled from Marlborough Down. They were used to construct five trilithons, each consisting of two upright stones and a linking horizontal stone. The trilithons were erected in a horseshoe shape and surrounded by a stone circle, the circle being surmounted by continuous lintels.

This was the main structure of Stonehenge for 500 years until, in 1600BC, an inner circle of Bluestones was added. In 1100BC, a 2.5 km (1.5 mile) avenue was constructed linking Stonehenge with the River Avon.

Most of the construction of Stonehenge was undertaken by the Beaker Folk and it obviously became the centre for their religious practices from 2100BC onwards, when the trilithons were raised and Avebury was abandoned. Dating from 2000BC onwards, there are more

Above: The round table, Winchester Castle.

than 200 round barrows within 16 km (10 miles) of Stonehenge. It seems that it became *the* area to be buried in!

We cannot be certain of the exact religious significance or purpose of Stonehenge but, for whatever reason, the Beaker Folk expended millions of man hours on its construction and it is the greatest remain of its period anywhere in Europe.

Alfred's Capital

Winchester is on the site of the Roman town *Venta Belgarum*, but its history really begins in the Dark Ages. Winchester's first cathedral, the Old Minster, was erected during the 7th century and, in the 9th century, Alfred the Great, King of Wessex (871–900), made it his capital. The city went on to become the capital of Saxon England and retained its position following William the Conqueror's arrival in 1066. About 100 years later, its status began to dwindle and London assumed the mantle, although Winchester remained a major centre of medieval England.

Norman Cathedral

The present Cathedral was started by the Normans in 1079, although their original central tower collapsed in 1107 and there was considerable alteration to the building in the 14th century. It is 169 m (556 ft) long, the longest medieval cathedral in Europe. The Library dates from 1150 and is the oldest book room in Europe. It contains the famous *Winchester Bible*, one of the finest illuminated bibles in the world.

Great Hall

The Normans also built one of their first post-Conquest castles in Winchester, with work commencing in 1067. The castle was destroyed, apart from its Great Hall, which was built by Henry III between 1222 and 1235 and is regarded as the second-best medieval hall in Britain, second only to Westminster Hall. Hanging in the Hall is reputed to be the top of King Arthur's Round Table but, disappointingly, tests show that it was constructed around 1335 (King Arthur supposedly lived in the 6th century).

Institutions

Winchester has two other major institutions from its great days. St. Cross Hospital was founded in 1136 and is the oldest of the almshouses in the country. Winchester College, founded in 1382, is the oldest public school in England.

Salisbury Cathedral

Salisbury Cathedral is unique amongst medieval city cathedrals. Most have been re-built over the centuries, always by the Normans and normally on Saxon or earlier foundations, often amongst the crowded streets of busy towns.

Salisbury is different. The old Cathedral was in Sarum, alongside a castle, but – at the start of the 13th century – the then Bishop decided that re-location should take place.

Depending on whom you believe, the site chosen was the result of a competition, negotiations with local landowners, or the place where the city's best archer's arrow landed when he shot it from the top of the existing Cathedral. The result was the building of a medieval 'greenfield site' cathedral 3.2 km (2 miles) south of the existing one (some archer!).

The Cathedral is also unique because the building of the main structure was completed in only 38 years, between 1220 and 1258, and it therefore represents a single architectural style – early English – rather than being the result of centuries of re-working.

Salisbury is special in a third way, in that the Cathedral Close was planned and enclosed by walls before other people started building around the Cathedral. Because of this, the greens around the Cathedral allow perfect views from all sides and, over the centuries, the Cathedral authorities have been able to control all building within the Close.

Finally, Salisbury Cathedral is unique in a fourth way – because of the only major feature that has been added to the main structure since 1258.

In 1335, it was decided that the Cathedral needed a spire to complete it. This decision was rather optimistic because the original builders had not structured the walls to carry such an additional weight and the ground that the Cathedral was built on is fairly waterlogged,

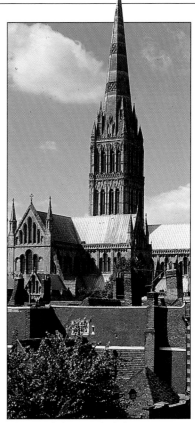

Above: Salisbury Cathedral.

but the spire was built and has been the Cathedral's crowning glory ever since. It stands 122.7 m (404 ft) tall and is the tallest in Britain. It weighs 6400 tons and its impact on the building can be judged by the way the walls have buckled slightly. In fact, the spire is slightly out of true but, after more than 600 years, the Cathedral authorities think it has finished settling.

A New Forest

William the Conqueror, having established himself in his new capital at Winchester, wanted somewhere to go hunting so, in 1079, he created a private hunting park, called *Nova Foresta*. It covered a huge area south from Winchester to the sea and west as far as the Dorset borders. The landscape was mixed but the foliage was mainly gorse and scrub.

William imposed very strict rules within his *Nova Foresta*, so that local people could not interfere with his land, the animals or the hunts. Some of his successors were keen hunters but increasingly, as the centuries passed, the emphasis within the area moved from hunting to forestation.

Oak trees were becoming increasingly important as a source of materials, particularly for shipbuilding, and an oak needed over 100 years to grow to the right size.

The New Forest of today is still protected as it was 900 years ago but is today much smaller, covering just 38332 ha (148 sq. miles) between Southampton and Ringwood. Oaks can still be found there but so can many other types of trees and there is also a controlled population of 1500 deer and 3000 ponies.

The need for oak timbers to build warships for the Royal Navy has disappeared, although in their heyday – during the 18th century – the shipyards at Buckler's Hard, on the edge of the Forest, built 50 mighty 'men-of-war', including the famous HMS *Agamemnon*, in 75 years. The Royal Navy, however, has not gone away. . .

Below: The Mary Rose*, Henry VIII's pride and joy.*

Be Prepared!

Westward of Portsmouth, just along the coast from Bournemouth, is Poole Harbour. It is similar to Portsmouth Harbour in that, after a narrow entrance, it opens into a broad anchorage. In fact, it is significantly larger than Portsmouth Harbour and is one of the largest natural harbours in the world. However, it is very shallow and totally unsuitable for large vessels so it has never been developed. Due to this, it is a haven for wildlife and very popular with sailing enthusiasts.

Located inside Poole Harbour is Brownsea Island. Low-lying and covered in woodland and heath, it is a nature reserve.

Lord Baden-Powell decided that Brownsea Island was perfect for his purposes and, in 1907, he took a group of 20 boys to a camp there – the Boy Scout movement was born.

Pompey

Look at any map of the Portsmouth area and you can see why it was inevitable that the city would become a naval base. The Solent is the stretch of water between the Isle of Wight and the English mainland. Approached from the east, the entrance to the Solent is guarded on the mainland side by Selsey Bill, Hayling Island, Portsmouth and Gosport. On the Isle, it is protected by Bembridge and Ryde.

Between Portsmouth and Gosport there is a narrow tidal opening that widens into a large triangular anchorage, with Portsmouth and Gosport forming the seaward 'jaws' and Porchester guarding the rear. One could not wish for a better defensive position. The Romans used the anchorage, and Porchester Castle is built into the corner of one of the Roman-Saxon Shore forts. The fort was built in the 3rd century AD and its preserved walls – at 5.5 m (18 ft) high and 3 m (10 ft) thick – are the best-preserved Roman fort walls in northern Europe.

More Forts

The Tudor kings, particularly Henry VIII, built castles both on the Isle of Wight and the mainland, and a fresh wave of fortification occurred in the 18th century in response to the Napoleonic threat of invasion. The most spectacular of these are four fortified platforms built as artificial islands off Bembridge, never used and now known as Palmerston's Follies.

Home of the Navy

The development of Portsmouth as a naval dockyard was started, essentially, by Henry VII, in 1495. His forebear, Henry V, had gathered his troops at Porchester, in 1415, to transport them to France and fight the Battle of Agincourt, but he boarded the troops at Southampton.

Henry VII fortified the harbour and built the first dry dock in Britain and, in 1540, Henry VIII made it the official home of his Royal Navy.

Above: HMS Warrior, *the first iron-hulled armoured warship.*

The town is full of associations with the Navy, and the shore establishments, museums and castles all tell their story. However, it is the ships that really matter and Portsmouth has three that tell its story.

The Mary Rose

Chronologically, the first of Portsmouth's great ships is the *Mary Rose*.

During Tudor times, English warships were generally fairly small vessels with English sea captains priding themselves on speed, manoeuvrability and skill. The *Mary Rose* was an exception. Weighing 700 tons and carrying 91 cannons, she had been re-built in 1536 and was Henry VIII's pride and joy. The King was present at Portsmouth in July 1545, when she put to sea with the rest of the fleet to face the French. A freak wind caught her sails, she keeled over and sank into the Solent without trace, resulting in the loss of 700 men.

The wreck lay where it had sunk for centuries, but its position was discovered in 1836 and some cannons were recovered. It was 're-discovered' in 1971.

After the 1971 discovery, a major salvage mission was embarked upon and the *Mary Rose* was finally lifted in 1982. Because she had sunk in soft mud, the ship and her contents were remarkably well-preserved and she is now housed in a special building at the Naval Base where she provides a remarkable insight into Henry VIII's navy.

HMS Victory

Ship number two is unique in that it was built in 1765 and is still in commission with the Royal Navy.

With 227 years of continuous service as a naval vessel, HMS *Victory* is the oldest commissioned ship in the world. She is now in dry dock at the Naval Base but, equally amazingly, she remained afloat until 1921, having been sea-going for more than 150 years. She is, of course, also famous as Admiral Nelson's flagship at the Battle of Trafalgar and the scene of his death. Indeed, *Victory* offers an accurate portrayal of life on a Royal Navy 'man-of-war' during the Napoleonic Wars.

HMS Warrior

The third vessel of note is HMS *Warrior*. Launched in 1860, she was the world's first iron-hulled armoured warship. She is the first real forerunner of the battleships and dreadnoughts and marked the end of the wooden-hulled warship.

Regarded as the ultimate fighting machine when she was launched, *Warrior* is also in the Naval Base and offers a rare insight into life in Queen Victoria's navy.

The South East

Gardens and Guardians, Invasions and Churches

The term 'the South East' is often used rather vaguely, but can be taken to mean what used to be called the Home Counties, or to include any part of the country where commuters to London live. In this Guide, the South East is restricted to the counties of Kent, Surrey and Sussex. This region covers an area often referred to as the 'Garden of England' and certainly includes many great gardens, ranging from the Royal Horticultural Society at Wisley to the National Trust at Claremont.

The region is also sometimes called the 'Gateway to England' and, at its closest point, is only just under 34 km (21 miles) from France. Because of this, it has been vulnerable to invasion and attempted invasion many times, and has been heavily fortified over the centuries. Well-preserved defences include castles and forts dating from Norman to Napoleonic times, the Royal Military Canal, and Martello Towers. The greatest of all these defences is Dover Castle and it has been recognised since Roman times that, if the region is the 'Gateway to England', then Dover is the 'Key to England'. The South East is also a major religious and educational centre, focused primarily on Canterbury, the mother church of Anglicans worldwide. It is also an area of leisure with resorts all along the coast.

Invasions

The White Cliffs of Dover and the coastline of Kent and Sussex must have seemed very inviting to people standing on the shore of mainland Europe or sailing through the English Channel over the millennia.

It appears that there were a number of incursions over the last few centuries BC because the Romans occupying Gaul were certainly aware of stories and legends about the land and people 'across the water'.

Roman Invaders

Julius Caesar was the first Roman to lead organised raids on England, landing first in 55BC, probably around Walmer or Deal, with two legions. However, the invasion met heavy opposition and he withdrew.

Caesar returned in 54BC with a larger and more organised force consisting of five legions transported in 800 vessels. He probably landed around Hythe and fought his way into the country. He is thought to have crossed the Thames at Brentford and withdrawn once more

Harold's death-spot, Battle Abbey.

Above: The White Cliffs of Dover.

after heavy fighting, but this time he did manage to extract tribute from the local tribal chieftains.

It was under the Roman Emperor Claudius that the decision was taken to invade Britain and establish a permanent presence. The invasion happened in 43AD and was led by Plautius with 20 000 men under his command. The first landings were again probably around the Hythe area.

Within 40 years, the southern half of England was firmly under Roman control with a network of headquarters, forts and roads, while the Governor, Agricola, was busy subduing northern England and venturing into Scotland. The Romans ruled England until the early 5th century AD when pressure on Rome forced the shrinking of the Empire and the abandonment of England to her own future.

Saxon Control

The next major invasion to centre on the region was in 449 when Hengist, Horsa and their Saxon warriors landed their longships at Pegwell Bay. The Saxons controlled the region, although not without conflict from the Vikings and Danes, until William the Conqueror arrived from Normandy.

Holy Invaders

A more peaceful 'invasion' occurred at Pegwell Bay in 597, when St. Augustine and his 40 monks landed with the mission to bring Christianity to the land.

The Battle of Hastings

The Battle of Hastings, or more accurately the Battle of Senlac Hill, occurred ten days after William of Normandy invaded. Harold commanded 10 000 troops and held a strong defensive position which William, with only 9000 troops, had to attack. The Battle was fierce and bloody, Norman losses were heavy and there is a theory that, if Harold had not been killed by an arrow, he may have succeeded in thwarting the assault. But it was not to be; William triumphed, and later, he had Battle Abbey erected on the battlesite. William soon appreciated the importance of the region and began work on castles and cathedrals to reinforce his control, particularly in Dover and Rochester.

Although 1066 marked the last successful military invasion, over the last 900 years England, and Great Britain, have many times been in dispute with the countries of mainland Europe. Time and time again, the threat of invasion of the country through the South East has caused concern and spates of military building and activity. The last unsuccessful 'invasion' – the Battle of Britain – was fought in the skies over the region.

Below: Sunset at Dover Castle.

Dover Castle

Dover's strategic position as an easily defensible harbour within striking distance of the Continent is clearly shown by its castle. It sits on top of the White Cliffs which rise 114 m (374 ft) from sea level. William the Conqueror built a motte and bailey fort to replace an earlier Saxon fortress, but most of the present structure was built by Henry II between 1180 and 1189, and was the first concentric castle in Britain. Predating its nearest rival by more than 100 years, it was also one of the earliest concentric castles in Europe and is one of the greatest. The fortifications consist of a massive Great Tower surrounded by an Inner Curtain Wall and then an Outer Curtain Wall.

The Great Tower is close to being a perfect cube, measuring 30 m (98 ft) by 29 m (96 ft) with walls 29 m (95 ft) high. The walls are 6.4 m (21 ft) thick at ground level, thinning to 5.2 m (17 ft) thick at battlement level.

In its own right, this is a major fortification but the Curtain Walls make the entire structure even more impressive. The Inner Curtain forms the first defensive ring round the Great Tower and includes 14 towers. The Outer Curtain

contains a total area of 13.74 ha (34 acres) and has 20 towers round its length, including the Norfolk Towers and Constable's Gate. The Norfolk Towers were built by King John as the main Gateway to the Castle but were undermined in 1216, and Henry III had them re-structured as a group of fortified towers. He also created a new Gateway and Barbican at Constable's Gate, one of the most elaborate castle gateways in Europe.

The Outer Curtain encloses three reminders of Dover's importance in even earlier days. The first is the remains of an iron-age fort which can be seen on the cliff top. The second, Pharos, is the tallest Roman remain in Britain. Originally a 24.5 m (80 ft) high tower topped by a beacon to guide shipping into the Roman harbour, the bottom 12 m (40 ft) are still standing alongside the third reminder, St. Mary-in-Castro, which was built in the 10th century as the church of the Saxon fortress.

Since 1216, Dover Castle has not been breached and it played an active role in the defence of the country until 1945.

The Castle protects the town and harbour from the North East, but it is not

Dover's only fortification. The area was also protected on the southwest side by the Western Heights Citadel, built as an additional defence during the period of fear about Napoleonic invasion. It now serves as a borstal but has one unique feature, the Grand Shaft. This is a 43 m (140 ft) long triple staircase linking the barracks and the town. It was built in 1809 to allow the troops rapid access to their defensive positions in the event of invasion.

Wall Paintings

Dover town itself also contains the Roman Painted House. This is a museum but it contains the remains of a Roman town house with wall paintings from the 2nd century AD, the oldest in Britain.

The Busiest Port

However, the town and port are definitely not preserved history. The present harbour has been created by a series of piers and breakwaters – the longest, Admiralty Pier, is 1220 m (4000 ft) long. The piers creating the Outer Harbour protect an area of 344 ha (1.33 sq. miles) and the port handles over 12 000 000 passengers per year, making it the busiest passenger port in Britain.

Canterbury

Twenty-four kilometres (15 miles) northwest of Dover, sitting astride the River Stour, is Canterbury.

Canterbury was already an established town by the time St. Augustine arrived in 597AD to begin his Christian mission. There is evidence of settlements in the area from the Iron Age onwards and the Romans established *Durovernum* as a major town on the route from London to the coastal ports. The city has a number of remains from the Roman period, including a famous mosaic pavement, and the current city walls were built on Roman foundations. It seems likely that early Roman Christianity reached Canterbury before the Romans deserted the country, as we know it reached Lullingstone in north Kent

Below: The Pharos, St. Mary-in-Castro.

Above: The armoured effigy of the Black Prince.

as St. Augustine's Abbey and its ruins are still visible outside the city walls to the west of the present Cathedral.

Around 600AD, Augustine established the King's School in Canterbury. It still exists and is the oldest school in Britain.

Then, in 603, Augustine declared Canterbury the centre of the Roman Church in England and himself Archbishop of Canterbury, although it was only after the Synod of Whitby, in 664, that the supremacy of the Roman Church was accepted throughout the country.

A Mighty Cathedral

The present Canterbury Cathedral was founded by the Normans in 1070 and was the work of Lanfranc, the first Norman Archbishop of Canterbury.

Above: Canterbury Cathedral.

Building work continued from 1070 until 1076 and, although little of the Norman building survives above ground, the crypt is the largest Norman crypt in the world. Lanfranc was also responsible for establishing the supremacy of Canterbury over York as the primary Archbishopric in England, and the 1072 documents certifying this are still held in the Cathedral archives.

There were two events in the 1170s that shaped the Cathedral into what we see today. The murder and subsequent martyrdom and sanctification of Archbishop Thomas à Becket in 1170 was followed by a disastrous fire in 1174, and the restored and re-built Cathedral

and as far inland and up-country as St. Albans, but there are no definite Christian relics in the city from the Roman period.

Augustine at Work

By the time St. Augustine reached Canterbury, it was the capital of Ethelbert, King of Kent. Ethelbert's wife, Berthaq, was French by birth and already a Christian. Her husband was still pagan but

had given her an old Roman building to use as a place of worship. St. Augustine took over the building and, when he had successfully converted Ethelbert, the King was baptised into Christianity. The building, now called St. Martin's Church, is still a place of worship and is the oldest church in England still in use.

The monastery established by Augustine's monks in 589AD became known

was enriched by a penitent Henry II and the millions of pilgrims who followed his path to Canterbury.

Building and decorative work at the Cathedral was started after the 1174 fire by William of Sens and continued for hundreds of years. The nave was completed in the 15th century, the central Bell Henry Tower in the 16th century, and the last tower, the North West, in 1840.

The Cathedral has suffered some despoiling over the centuries, particularly the destruction of Becket's magnificent tomb in 1538 on the orders of Henry VIII, but most of the fabric is still intact.

The stained glass is magnificent and includes some fine examples of rare 12th-century work. Finally, the statues and memorials complete the overall majesty of the building. They include the tombs of more than 50 Archbishops

Above: Knole House.

of Canterbury, but the finest memorial is that of the Black Prince, who died in 1376. His armoured effigy is regarded by many as the finest in Britain.

Canterbury Cathedral is the Mother Church of Anglicans worldwide and continues to be as popular with visitors from around the world as it was with pilgrims in Chaucer's day. In 1990, there were 2 250 000 of them.

Noble Homes

The South East has always been a favourite region for homes of the nobility and the famous. The combination of its proximity to London and the coast, coupled with its mild climate and pleasant landscape, have long been prized. Two examples – separated by almost 1500 years – demonstrate this.

Fishbourne

Fishbourne is close to the Sussex coast near Chichester. In 1960, some workmen found a few remains, a discovery that led to the uncovering of a masterpiece of Roman building. They had hit upon what was eventually revealed to be a Roman palace. It is the largest Roman building so far revealed in Britain and is literally an example of Imperial Rome at its best, transplanted in England.

Above: Roman remains at Fishbourne.

The building was very formal and consisted of four wings built around ornamental gardens of box hedges. One wing contained official reception rooms, a second the owner's accommodation,

A Very Large Hole

Over the centuries, many have dreamed of closing the sea gap between Britain and mainland Europe. Some envisaged chains of bridges linked to artificial islands built in the Channel, others sinking huge tubes under the water and chaining them on the sea-bed. The really ambitious thought of tunnels, with the first major plan put forward in 1802 by Albert Mathieu-Favier.

Over the last 200 years, many plans have been drawn up and, on one occasion, excavation work commenced. However, each plan was shelved because of problems ranging from the threat of war to health scares but – most often of all – because of costs.

Finally, on 12 February, 1986, the British and French governments signed agreements allowing private investors to create companies to build and run the Channel Tunnel. Construction work started on 1 July, 1987, while the first linking of the tunnels occurred on 30 October, 1990, and today all three tunnels are fully excavated. There are two rail tunnels, one in each direction, and a service tunnel with cross-links to both main tunnels. The first passenger trains should run through the tunnels in mid-to-late 1993.

Tunnel statistics are, naturally, impressive. The Channel Tunnel is the second longest tunnel in the world; the distance between the two portals is 49.94 km (31.03 miles). Thirty-seven kilometres (23 miles) of this is under the Channel and the maximum depth reached below the sea-bed is 70 m (230 ft). Excavating the three tunnels generated 6 700 000 m³ (246 000 000 cu. ft) of spoil.

By the time the first trains run, the total expenditure on the Channel Tunnel will have reached £9 000 000 000, but it will take a mere 35 minutes to get from Kent to France.

a third accommodation for visiting Imperial dignitaries and the fourth accommodation for less important visitors. The remains of heating systems, mosaic floors and marble and stucco wall-coverings emphasise the importance of the owner. It must have been the home of either the Roman Governor of the Province or one of the pro-Roman Kings who controlled their kingdoms for the Roman invaders. It was also constructed very shortly after the invasion, probably around 50AD. Most experts agree that it was almost certainly the home of Cogidubnus, King of the Regni. Fishbourne Roman Palace was occupied until about 280AD when there is evidence that it burnt down.

Knole

In 1456, Bourchier, Archbishop of Canterbury, began to construct a new house at Knole. It remained the property of the Archbishops until Cranmer was persuaded to 'give' it to Henry VIII in 1538, and in 1566, Elizabeth I gave it to the Sackville family. Thomas Sackville started re-building and extension work to the house in 1603, and the family obviously had a preoccupation with size and the calendar. As completed by Thomas, the house had 365 rooms, one for each day of the year, and 52 staircases, one for each week of the year. Knole House is still the house with the largest number of rooms in Britain.

Three Gardens

Sissinghurst

A descendent of the Sackvilles of Knole was the writer, Vita Sackville-West, who died in 1962. Together with husband and fellow writer, Harold Nicolson, she created a remarkable garden in the grounds of Sissinghurst Castle. They began work in 1930 – he planned and she planted – and it is now looked after by the National Trust and is one of the most-visited gardens in Britain.

Above: The lake at Claremont.

Wisley

Another popular garden is at Wisley in Surrey. It is owned by the Royal Horticultural Society and its 100 ha (350 acres) contain RHS displays and samples on all forms of gardening from woodlands to vegetable gardens.

Claremont

Also in Surrey is the Claremont Landscape Garden. It is now cared for by the National Trust and was created from 1711 for Thomas Pelham. The initial work carried out between 1711 and 1726 was undertaken by Bridgeman and Vanbrugh and included the creation of a lake and Bridgeman's great turf amphitheatre. In 1727, it was described as 'the noblest garden in Europe' and, soon after, William Kent and Capability Brown were brought in to continue its development. Both of them retained Bridgeman's natural approach whilst introducing their own features. Claremont Landscape Garden has now been restored and is the earliest 'natural-English' landscape garden in the country.

Left: Sissinghurst Gardens.

Prince Regent's Delight

Brighton began to develop in the mid-18th century after Dr. Richard Russell, a local resident, published his book, *A Dissertation Concerning The Use Of Sea Water In Diseases Of The Glands*. Its publication was one of the major factors in persuading people to 'take the waters'.

The resort's success was guaranteed when the Prince of Wales visited in 1783 and gave it the royal seal of approval by deciding to build a house in the town. In 1787, he commissioned Henry Holland to construct the original house for him, and Holland built a large but fairly straightforward seaside villa.

The Prince of Wales became the Prince Regent and then George IV and, through these changes, his needs, and the entourage travelling with him, grew. In 1815, he commissioned John Nash to enlarge the villa. This Nash duly did and, by 1822, he had not only increased the size, he had also restructured the entire building and added domes and minarets to the roofs. The Royal Pavilion had been created. It is a unique

Above: Europe's largest man-made marina – Brighton.

structure; externally, it resembles someone's dream of an Indian moghul's palace and, internally, the designs and furnishings emphasise dragons, pagodas and oriental vistas and 'transport' you to the Imperial Chinese Court.

Popular Pier

Brighton's popularity remains undiminished. The Palace Pier was constructed in 1899 and is the archetypal Victorian seaside pier, with rides, amusements, shows and, in its case, the smallest barber's shop in the world. In 1990, it attracted 3 500 000 visitors, making it the most popular seaside pier in the country.

Superlatives Old and New

Volk's Electric Railway runs eastwards from the Palace Pier. It first opened in 1883 and is the oldest electric railway in Britain. In fact, it runs eastwards towards Brighton's latest superlative, the Marina. Opened in 1978, it is Europe's largest man-made marina, and can hold more than 2000 boats. It also houses shops, entertainments and restaurants.

Below: The Royal Pavilion, Brighton.

Entertaining London

The Great Tourist Attractions, Including a Maze, a Zoo and a Waxworks

London is a major cultural centre and the home of most of the country's national museums and art collections. Between them, the British Museum, National Gallery, Victoria & Albert Museum, Tate Gallery and others contain some of the finest collections in the world.

But entertainment and leisure in London is not confined to these great national treasures. Londoners enjoy some of the finest gardens in the country, particularly at Kew and Hampton Court.

The Zoological Society of London in Regent's Park runs the oldest public zoo in the world.

Londoners can enjoy a wide range of spectator sports, often at stadia with superb facilities – Wembley is the greatest of these. Used for Britain's last Olympic Games (1948), the main stadium is still the largest in Britain with all-covered seating.

London's theatreland has a rich history which started with the great Elizabethan theatres of Southwark. The exact locations of these theatres, famous as the setting for the first performances of many of Shakespeare's plays, were lost for centuries but fortunately, in the 1980s, they were discovered.

London's inns and pubs are often ancient and rich in history, none more so than The Dove in Hammersmith.

Madame Tussaud reached London at the start of the 19th century, having been forced to make death masks of victims of the French Revolution. They became the basis of her original exhibitions around Britain, and today Tussauds is the most popular waxworks in the world and one of London's great tourist attractions.

Above: Kew Gardens.

Two Gardens

Royal Botanic Gardens

Kew is the home of the Royal Botanic Gardens. The present gardens cover 116 ha (288 acres) and have expanded from the original gardens created in 1759 for Princess Augusta, wife of Frederick, Prince of Wales.

Over the centuries, plants and trees have been collected from across the world, studied and nurtured by Kew's scientists and often re-distributed to other countries for commercial production. Two classic examples of this are the Rubber Tree and Captain Bligh's famous Breadfruit.

Nowadays, there are around 25 000 different plant species in the collection, including more than 3000 that are kept sheltered in Kew's famous conservatories. The collection includes the oldest pot plant in the world, a single cycad called *Encephalartos altensteinii*. It was brought to Kew from South Africa in

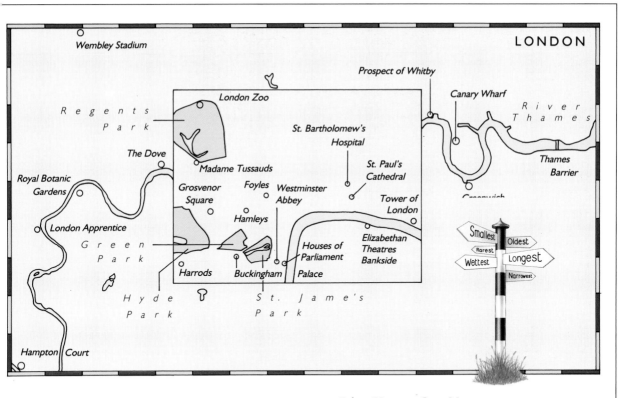

LONDON

Wembley Stadium

Prospect of Whitby

Canary Wharf

River Thames

London Zoo

Regents Park

St. Bartholomew's Hospital

The Dove

St. Paul's Cathedral

Madame Tussauds

Royal Botanic Gardens

Grosvenor Square

Foyles

Westminster Abbey

Tower of London

London Apprentice

Green Park

Hamleys

Houses of Parliament

Elizabethan Theatres Bankside

Harrods

Buckingham

Palace

Thames Barrier

Greenwich

Hyde Park

St. James's Park

Smallest Oldest
Rarest
Wettest Longest
Narrowest

Hampton Court

Below: Hampton Court Maze.

1775 and is still growing. It is probably also the rarest pot plant in the world and might be a hybrid of a palm-like tropical cycad *Encephalartos woodii*, a plant that has existed on earth for over 200 million years, the only known specimen of which is also at Kew.

Two of Kew's conservatories were designed by Decimus Burton. The Palm House, which was completed in 1848, and the larger Temperate House which opened in 1899. The Temperate House encloses 5209 m² (48 392 sq. ft) and is one of the largest glasshouses in Britain.

The Gardens contain many features and follies. The two most famous are the Pagoda and the Flagstaff. The Pagoda was built in 1761 and, at 50 m (163 ft), is the tallest in Britain. The Flagstaff is provided for the Gardens by Canada. The present one was erected on 7 May, 1958, and at 68 m (225 ft) tall, is the tallest flagstaff in Britain.

Hampton Court

Hampton Court Gardens surround the Tudor mansion built by Cardinal Wolsey in 1514 and 'given' by him to Henry VIII in 1529. The house used to be the

Waxworks

Madame Marie Tussaud was already an experienced wax-model maker working in Paris when she was ordered by the leaders of the French Revolution to make models of the death masks of the aristocrats killed with the guillotine.

In 1802, she moved to England, bringing her models and heads with her, and she set up a touring exhibition of her work.

In 1833, she decided to develop a permanent home for her waxworks in London, initially in Baker Street and, from 1884 onwards, at the present site in Marylebone Road.

Madame Tussaud's is now the most popular waxworks in the world and, along with its neighbour, the London Planetarium, it is one of the greatest tourist attractions in the capital with even more paying visitors than the Tower of London, averaging above 2 500 000 a year.

The Zoo

The Zoological Society of London was founded in 1826 by, amongst others, Sir Stamford Raffles and Sir Humphrey Davy. Private menageries and zoos, particularly royal collections, existed long before this but the London Zoo was the world's first public collection. The original site in Regent's Park was laid out by Decimus Burton in 1827 and was opened to the public for the first time on 27 April, 1828.

The Regent's Park site covers 14.5 ha (36 acres) and the Society also owns the much larger Whipsnade Park in Bedfordshire. Whipsnade was opened on 23 May, 1931, and covers 219 ha (541 acres).

Conservation

After much controversy and uncertainty during the 1980s and early '90s, the Society's future appears secure and the premises in Regent's Park will continue to be used, although the emphasis will change to conservation and protection, with the majority of the animals housed at Whipsnade. Across the two sites, the Society currently looks after more than 10 000 specimens.

Below: The Prospect of Whitby.

largest royal residence in Britain. Both it and its gardens have many fascinating and historic features, the two best-known being the Maze and the Great Vine.

Hampton Court Maze is the oldest hedge maze in Britain. It was created by George London and Henry Wise in 1690, although it has been re-designed over the years. The present complicated trapezoid of yew hedges covers an area measuring 67.66 m (222 ft) by 24.99 m (82 ft).

The Great Vine at Hampton Court is England's largest. It was planted in 1768 and has a girth of 215.9 cm (85 in) with branches 34.7 m (114 ft) long. It yields an average of 318.8 kg (703 lbs) of black grapes every year.

Wembley

The Wembley Complex includes Wembley Arena and the Wembley Conference Centre but is most famous for the twin-towered Empire Stadium. Built in 1923, it hosted the 1948 Olympic Games and was the site of England's 1966 World Cup triumph.

It is also the venue for each year's FA Cup Final and all the England team's home games. Its terraces can hold 100 000 spectators and it is the largest covered stadium in Britain.

The Dove

London has many historic inns, most of which are scattered along the River Thames from The Prospect of Whitby in Wapping to The London Apprentice in Isleworth.

One of the most famous is The Dove on the riverside at Hammersmith. Whilst it is not the oldest riverside inn (that honour goes to The Prospect of Whitby which was founded in 1520), it does have a rich history. Charles II and Nell Gwynne used to meet there; the designer William Morris once lived a few doors away, A.P. Herbert, the writer and humorist, said it was his favourite pub, James Thomson composed *Rule Britannia* in the bar and I had my stag night there!

The Dove has a front bar that measures only 126 cm (4 ft 2 in) by 239 cm (7 ft 10 in), making it the smallest bar in Britain.

Shakespeare's Theatres

Bankside in Southwark was famous as the home of the great Elizabethan theatres. These spectacular, galleried theatres in the round were as much a part of the entertainment as the plays themselves.

The two most famous were the Globe and the Rose. The Rose was the first to be built, in 1587, followed by the Globe in 1599, and both had been destroyed by the middle of the 17th century.

Excavation

After much painstaking work, the site of the Globe was finally uncovered in the early 1980s and work is now well underway to build a full-size replica of the original theatre that, later on this decade, will once again be a venue for the lost theatrical style of Shakespeare and his contemporaries.

In 1989, during excavations for a new office block, the foundations of the equally important Rose were also uncovered. Archeologists studied the finds and the remains are now preserved under the offices.

Below: Wembley Stadium.

The Thames Barrier, the world's largest movable flood barrier.

Commercial London

From a Flood Barrier to a Shopaholic's Dream

In addition to being the capital city of England, London is also the prime commercial and financial centre of Britain and the commercial sector has created many of London's greatest and most famous landmarks.

Over the centuries, one of London's problems has been its position astride the River Thames. The Thames Estuary acts as a type of funnel for the North Sea, and storms and high tides could cause surges bringing flood water into the heart of the city. To overcome this problem, the Thames Flood Barrier was erected in the 1970s and '80s.

Many visitors to Britain fly into the country and the majority of them arrive at London Heathrow, almost a city in its own right and the busiest international airport in the world.

There is less pressure on land space in London than, for example, in New York's Manhattan, but some developers still want to build high, recent and spectacular examples being Olympia and York at Canary Wharf in London's Docklands.

Although it is not strictly speaking a commercial building, the majority of visitors to the United States Embassy in London go there for commercial reasons and when they do so they enter the largest building of its type in Britain.

There are many ways of getting around London, including walking, using the ubiquitous London black cabs, the world-famous red double decker buses and the underground tube system, the first of its kind in the world.

Shopping is one of London's pleasures and amongst the wide range of shops you can visit are Britain's largest department store and the world's largest record shop, book shop and toy shop.

High-flying Heathrow

To the west of London is Heathrow Airport – the largest and most important airport in Britain with 51 400 employees.

Heathrow was built as an airplane testing base in 1929, became a fighter base during World War II and was converted for civilian use in 1946. It first exceeded 1 000 000 passengers in a year in 1953.

Plane Facts

Nowadays, there are 70 airlines from 61 countries flying into Heathrow and, in 1990, the airport handled 344 841 passenger flights involving the movement of 39 610 550 people. Of these, 31 525 476 passengers were on international flights, making Heathrow the busiest international airport in the world.

The Barrier

Creating the Thames Barrier, the world's largest movable flood barrier, was the solution to safeguarding the centre of London from flooding whilst leaving the city accessible to ships.

In normal water conditions, all that can be seen of the Thames Barrier are nine mighty piers. Each pier is clad in stainless steel and looks like a humpbacked whale or the curved prow of a boat.

Hidden on the riverbed are the gates that link each pier, and in emergencies the gates are rotated through 90° to stand upright, lock into each of the piers and form an impenetrable barrier 20 m (66 ft) tall. The total barrier is 555 m (1830 ft) long with six 61 m (200 ft) wide gates and two 31.3 m (103 ft) wide gates. The large gates each weigh 1300 tons.

Pleasure Trips

The Thames Barrier was planned in 1971; work commenced in 1974. It was officially opened in 1984 and has become a major tourist attraction, with Thames pleasure boats making trips down river and through the barrier.

Canary Wharf

The Canary Wharf office complex is one of the key developments in the regeneration of London's Docklands.

Towering Over London

It covers 29 ha (71 acres) of formerly derelict docks on the Isle of Dogs and its centrepiece is the Tower.

Designed by Caesar Pelli, the 50-storey Tower is 244 m (800 ft) tall, the tallest building in Britain and the second tallest in Europe. It is clad in stainless steel around a framework constructed from 16 000 pieces of steel weighing 27 000 tons. It is supported by 212 deep piles topped by a massive concrete raft, and the entire construction took just 3 years to build.

Grosvenor Square

The front of the United States Embassy occupies the whole of one side of Grosvenor Square and is dominated by a 3m (9 ft) tall eagle with an 11 m (35 ft) wingspan.

Largest Embassy

The main building occupies seven floors, three of which are below ground, and contains 600 rooms with a usable floorspace of 236 895 m² (2 550 000 sq. ft). It was completed in 1960 and is the largest embassy in Britain.

Going Underground

The London Underground Railway was the first city centre rapid transit train system to be developed in the

world. The first purpose-built section was from Paddington to Farringdon Street and it opened on 10 January, 1863, and is now part of the Metropolitan Line.

The first deep tube train ran from the Tower of London to Bermondsey in 1869.

Tunnel Vision

The present system runs 478 trains around 409 km (254 miles) of track with 272 stations. The network employs 19 000 people and, in 1990, carried 765 000 000 passengers. The longest continuous tunnel on the network runs for 27.84 km (17½ miles) between Morden and East Finchley and is the longest rail tunnel in Britain and the third longest in the world.

Shopping Around

Harrod's

Henry Charles Harrod had little idea that he was founding Britain's largest department store when he started a modest grocery shop in 1849.

Above: Canary Wharf.

The shop prospered and expanded, most notably after a fire in 1884 and a major re-fit and extension in 1901–5.

In 1889, the first escalators in Britain were installed there, with an attendant at the top offering either brandy or smelling salts to terrified shoppers!

In 1902, the famous Food Halls were created with their listed tiled ceilings and walls, including The Hunt, created for the Meat Hall by the Royal Doulton Company.

Harrods has become an institution and the latest statistics tell the story very

Left: The American Embassy.

Hamleys

Occupying 4180 m² (45 000 sq. ft) of selling space spread over six floors, and including play areas and displays of model trains, Hamleys is the largest toy shop in the world.

Although founded in 1760 in premises in Holborn, Hamley's moved to Regent Street in 1901 where, particularly in the weeks leading up to Christmas, it is a mecca for children of all ages.

Foyles

Foyles Bookshop was founded in 1906 by the two Foyle brothers and is run today by Christina Foyle. The store on Charing Cross Road carries a stock of approximately 6 000 000 books displayed on 48 km (30 miles) of shelving built over five floors, and – in terms of stock carried – it is the largest bookshop in the world.

HMV

Record lovers will find a warm welcome at the HMV store in Oxford Street. It was opened on 24 October, 1986, and the trading floors cover 3408 m² (36 684 sq. ft) making it the largest record shop in the world.

well. It has 200 departments and employs between 4000 and 5000 staff dependent upon the time of year. It has 9 ha (22 acres) of selling space and its record turnover for one year was £312 000 000 in 1986–7. The record one-day take for the first day of the famous Harrods Sale is £7 000 000.

Below: Harrods – 22 acres of selling space.

Historic London

From a Famous Cathedral to a 15th-Century Palace and a River Race

Understandably, given its dual role as both the nation's capital and largest city, London is steeped in history. Many buildings, particularly in Westminster and the City, have played major roles in the shaping of Britain.

Amongst these, a significant number are worthy of the designation 'superlative', and in this section on Historic London most of them reflect the roles of the Church and the Crown over the centuries.

St. Paul's Cathedral in the City is the finest of Christopher Wren's works and the only domed cathedral in Britain. It also has the largest crypt in Europe.

Westminster the Abbey is the largest church in Britain and has been the setting for the coronation of every crowned English monarch since William the Conqueror in 1066.

The only part of the original Palace of Westminster still standing is William II's Westminster Hall, a building with the greatest roof in England and the scene of some of the most important trials in British history, including that of Charles I. On the edge of Westminster is Buckingham Palace, the London residence of the monarch and the largest palace in Britain.

Back in the City, William the Conqueror built his great tower to subdue the citizens, and further down river in Greenwich is probably the finest collection of 17th- and 18th-century buildings in the country.

St. Bartholomew's Hospital at Smithfield is the second oldest hospital in the country and has remained on the same site since its foundation in the early 12th century.

Doggett's Coat and Badge is a fascinating annual race for Thames watermen. It was first held in 1715, pre-dates the famous Oxford and Cambridge University Boat Race by more than a century and is the oldest river race in the country.

Wren's Cathedral

There has been a church on the site of the present St. Paul's since the 6th century. The first Saxon church was burnt down during the 11th century. The Norman replacement became known as Old St. Paul's and its construction continued sporadically between 1087 and the 14th century.

It was a very large building, 178 m (585 ft) long, with a spire erected in 1315 that was 148 m (484 ft) high – 24 m (80 ft) higher than Salisbury Cathedral's spire – and dominated the winding streets and alleys of the City. Unfortunately, by the 17th century, it had fallen into disrepair and architects Inigo Jones and Christopher Wren were asked to look at ways of refurbishing it.

Then, on 2 September, 1666, a fire in a baker's shop in Pudding Lane changed the City forever. The Great Fire of London destroyed 87 churches, 44 livery halls and more than 13 000 houses. It severely damaged Old St. Paul's and kept Christopher Wren busy for the rest of his life! The original suggestion was that the old cathedral should be rebuilt, but fortunately Wren disagreed and had the ruins demolished.

His early designs were all rejected as too revolutionary until, in 1675, he submitted a third revised design. This was a compromise to gain approval and undoubtedly Wren never intended to build it. It was approved, but he had formally agreed that he was allowed to make modifications as required whilst work was underway.

The first stone was laid on 21 June, 1675, and the last part of the dome was completed in 1710, by which time Wren was 78 years old. His masterpiece is 156 m (513 ft) long, 37 m (123 ft) wide across the nave, 54 m (179 ft) wide across the west front and 111 m (365 ft) high to the top of the cross surmounting

Opposite: The Palace of Westminster.

the dome. Wren's tomb in St. Paul's tells its own story. Translated, the inscription says: 'Reader, if you seek his monument, look around you.'

The dome is an amazing construction and in fact, St. Paul's is the only domed cathedral in Britain and has the third largest cathedral dome in the world. The major problem with a dome is that if the dimensions fit in artistically with the interior of the building, then the exterior looks stranger and overly small, and vice versa. To overcome this, Wren built three domes for St. Paul's.

The inner dome blends perfectly with the interior of the Cathedral whilst the lead-covered outer dome is in scale with the exterior grandeur. Between the two, the third dome of bricks supports the weight of the lantern and cross above the dome. The combined weight of the three domes is 64 000 tons and it is part of Wren's genius that it is supported by only eight piers.

The crypt is unique in that it occupies the same floorspace as the ground-floor

Above: St. Paul's – Britain's only domed cathedral.

plan of the entire cathedral, and it is the largest crypt in Europe. In addition to Wren's tomb, it contains the resting places of great painters, such as Turner and Reynolds, and the impressive tombs of the Duke of Wellington and Admiral Lord Nelson.

Edward the Confessor's Church

The Collegiate Church of St. Peter, Westminster, is more commonly referred to as Westminster Abbey. It is not a cathedral, although Henry VIII granted

Below: Westminster Abbey.

it such status for a time so that it was not affected by the Dissolution.

The Abbey is mthe largest church in Britain, having a total exterior length of 161 m (530 ft). The nave is 50 m (166 ft) long, 22 m (72 ft) wide and 31 m (102 ft) high and is the tallest in Britain.

There is evidence that a monastery or abbey has been on the site since around AD620, and Edward the Confessor started building his church for St. Peter in 1050. It was dedicated on 28 December, 1065, and Edward was buried in his Abbey on 6 January the following year.

Crowning Glory

The year of 1066 brought the Norman invasion and the end of Saxon rule, and William the Conqueror consolidated his power by having himself crowned in Westminster Abbey on Christmas Day, setting a precedent that has continued to this day. Every English and British monarch since William has been crowned in the Abbey (with the exception of Edward V, who died before he could be crowned, and Edward VIII, who abdicated).

The Tower

Whilst William the Conqueror was fully aware of the power of the Church, he was equally aware of the force of arms. Once safely crowned at Westminster Abbey, he started building a fortress downstream to keep the inhabitants of the City of London under control. He chose a site just outside the old Roman walls and created a fortified earthwork during 1067.

In 1078, construction started on a stone tower to further strengthen the fortress. The White Tower, as it later became known, was completed by 1097 and is a rectangle 36 m (118 ft) by 32 m (107 ft) rising 27 m (90 ft) into the air with corner towers rising a further 7.6 m (25 ft).

Further Expansion

From the 13th century onwards, Henry III and his son, Edward I, continued the fortification and expansion of the Tower. Henry built an inner curtain wall with 13 towers to surround the White Tower, and Edward built an outer curtain wall with six towers to surround the inner wall and create a perfect concentric fortification. Around the outer wall, he created a moat ranging between 23 m (75 ft) and 38 m (125 ft) wide with the River Thames on the south side.

Millions of Visitors

The Tower of London has had many functions over the centuries, including serving as a royal residence, home of the crown jewels, museum, zoo, prison and place of execution. It rivals Dover Castle as the most powerful fortification in Britain and, because of its position on the doorstep of the City, it is probably the best-known castle in the world. In 1990, it attracted a staggering 2 300 000 visitors.

The Palace of Westminster

The Normans were also busy building in Westminster. Edward the Confessor had started work on a palace for himself at the same time as he commenced Westminster Abbey, and the Normans continued the work, particularly William II, who built the great hall

Doggett's Coat and Badge

Over the centuries, the River Thames was normally the fastest, safest and most convenient means of transport for the rich and powerful, and the Thames Watermen developed into a powerful guild.

Thomas Doggett was an actor and comedian and manager of the Drury Lane Theatre. On one journey up river he was tremendously impressed by the skill and strength of the waterman who rowed him against the current to his destination.

In fact, he was so impressed that he decided to organise a competition restricted to watermen. The six selected rowers had to race from Old Swan Pier at London Bridge to the Old White Swan Inn in Chelsea, against the current for a distance of 7.2 km (4½ miles). The race was held on 1 August, 1715, and the winner received a silver badge and a red livery, Doggett's Coat and Badge.

The race then occurred annually until Doggett's death in 1721, and in his will he left a sum of money to purchase property, the income from which was to pay for the race and the prizes.

Doggett's Coat and Badge has been raced every year since, although it was suspended during both World Wars. However, it was run six times in 1919 and seven times in 1946 to catch up. It is the oldest boat race in Britain.

Above: St. Katharine's Dock and Tower.

which was completed in 1097. In 1265, the hall was the seat of Simon de Montfort's historic parliament.

Fires in 1299, 1512 and 1834 eventually led to the destruction of the Palace, with the exception of the great hall, and the present Houses of Parliament were constructed after the 1834 fire.

Raising the Roof

Richard II wanted the great hall rebuilt to improve its usefulness. The original Norman hall had a very large floor area, measuring 73 m (240 ft) by 21 m (69 ft), but the columns supporting the roof interrupted it and Richard commissioned a new single-span roof and the removal of the obstructive columns. The resulting double-hammerbeam roof, at a height of 27 m (90 ft), is the largest medieval single-span roof in England and one of the most beautiful in the world.

Great Trials

Westminster Hall has been used for banquets and state occasions – including the lying-in-state of great leaders – and, over the centuries, it has hosted some of the most important trials in the country, including those of Sir Thomas More, Guy Fawkes and, in 1649, the trial of King Charles I by Parliament.

Buckingham Palace

Over the centuries, English and British monarchs have had their favourite houses around the capital and these have included the Palaces of Westminster, Whitehall, Richmond, Hampton Court and Greenwich. Buckingham Palace became a royal residence relatively recently.

The site of the Palace was a mulberry garden until 1703, when it was purchased by John Sheffield, Duke of Buckingham, as the site on which to build his London home.

Re-construction

Buckingham House was purchased by George III in 1762 for the sum of £21 000, and was re-constructed as a Palladian-style palace between 1825 and 1836, with the east front added in 1846. The east front is 186 m (610 ft) long and was re-surfaced with Portland Limestone in 1912.

The Palace contains 600 rooms, including a 34 m (111 ft) long ballroom, and is the largest royal palace in Britain. Its gardens cover 15.8 ha (39 acres), including 2 ha (5 acres) of lakes.

Greenwich Palace

Greenwich Palace was built in 1427 and became a very popular royal residence during Tudor times, particularly with Henry VIII. Henry was born at Greenwich in 1491, as were his two daughters, the future Queens Mary, born in 1516, and Elizabeth, born in 1533.

Perfect Vistas

The Palace fell into disuse during the 17th century. Charles II was going to re-build it, but instead Christopher Wren was commissioned to build a Royal Naval Hospital. The resulting collection of four buildings-and their visual links with the buildings of the National Maritime Museum and, on the hill beyond them, the Royal Observatory-presents one of the most perfect architectural vistas in Britain and is a fitting tribute to the great architects who worked on it. The collection represents some of the finest work of Wren, Inigo Jones, John Webb, John Vanbrugh and Nicholas Hawksmoor.

Thornhills Masterpiece

The interiors of Greenwich Palace are equally impressive, culminating in the Painted Hall in King William's Block. Here, the ceiling is the largest painting in Britain. Called *The Triumph of Peace*, it is by Sir James Thornhill, measures 32.3 m (106 ft) by 15.4 m (51 ft) and took 20 years from 1707 to complete.

Barts

The first hospital in London, St. Bartholomew's was founded in 1123 and is pre-dated in Britain only by the foundation of St. Peter's in York. Uniquely, whilst it has been re-built on a number of occasions, 'Bart's' still stands on the original site of its creation nearly 870 years ago.

Below: Royal residence – Buckingham Palace.

Thames and Chilterns

From Roman Remains to an Ambitious New Town

The Thames and Chiltern region covers the counties immediately west and northwest of London ranging from affluent London commuter suburbs to rural Oxfordshire. The only geographical features of any real note are the Chiltern Hills and the River Thames.

The Thames is the longest river wholly within England. It rises in Gloucestershire but most of its 354 km (215 miles) length is within this region. Many of the Thameside towns and villages have played an important part in the history of England, particularly Oxford, Eton and Windsor.

The northern part of the region traces its importance back to Roman times, and there are stately homes throughout the area. The area also includes Milton Keynes, Britain's largest and most ambitious new town, a number of famous film studios and Bekonscot.

The City of Dreaming Spires

The rivers Thames and Cherwell meet 90 km (56 miles) northwest of central London, between the Chiltern Hills and the Cotswolds. The city that developed around the confluence is Oxford.

Exactly when a settlement first developed there is unclear. The ford may have been used in pre-historic times but it was ignored by the Romans, probably because it was an unhealthy site, wet and surrounded by hills. The first authenticated reference to Oxford was in the *Anglo Saxon Chronicles,* in 912.

Oxford University

By the time of the compilation of the Domesday Book, Oxford had become a religious centre with a number of churches and more than 100 properties in the town recorded as being owned by the Church. This concentration of religious buildings was bound to attract scholars to the town, although the precise date of the foundation of the University is again unclear. However, the expulsion of English students from Paris and their decision to move to Oxford to continue their studies is generally regarded as the date of foundation. This was in 1167 and makes Oxford the oldest university in Britain.

(Interestingly enough, it was unrest in Oxford, in 1209, that led some students to migrate to Cambridge to found Britain's second university.)

The college and university buildings dominate the centre of Oxford and a walk around the city will reveal the full glory of the centuries of building, but the following superlatives are particularly worthy of note . . .

The Bodlean Library was founded with a bequest of 2000 books by Sir Thomas Bodley, in 1602, to replace the earlier collections of Cobham and Duke Humphrey, which were dispersed during the Reformation. It is the oldest

Left: Blenheim Palace.

Above: The Botanic Gardens, Oxford University.

library in Britain and now contains more than 4 000 000 books.

Elias Ashmole donated his collection of curiosities to the University to form the basis of a museum. Using his accumulation, the Ashmolean Museum was founded as the first museum in Britain. It opened in 1683.

Wadham College is the location of the Holywell Music Room. It was first used in 1748 and is the oldest concert hall in Britain that is still in use.

Henry Danvers, Earl of Danby, created the University's Physic Garden in 1621. The Oxford University Botanic Gardens occupy the same site to this day

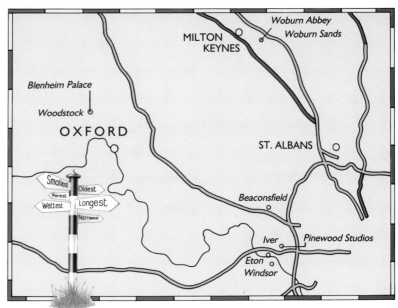

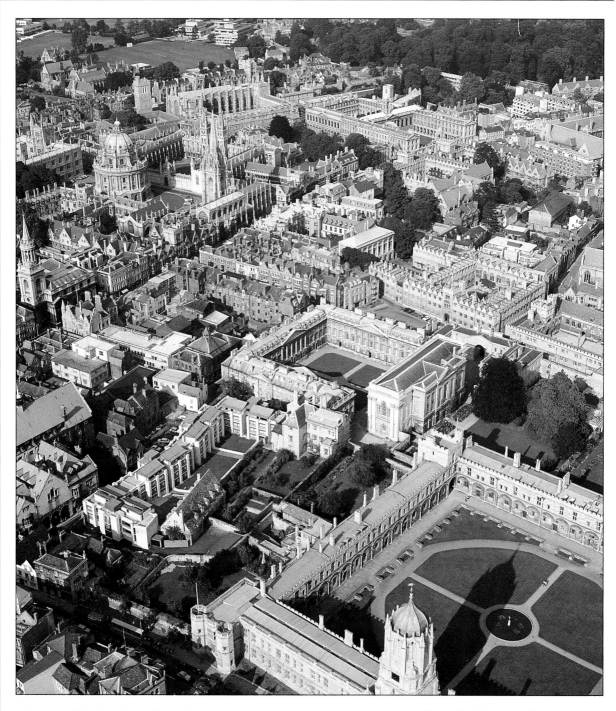

Above: Oxford – an aerial view.

and are the oldest botanic gardens in the country.

Oxford Cathedral

Oxford Cathedral is also worth mentioning. Christ Church has, since 1546, simultaneously been the cathedral of the bishopric of Oxford and the chapel of Christ Church College. It is also the smallest cathedral in England.

St. Albans

The Romans may have ignored the Oxford area, but they were as active in the north of the Thames and Chiltern region as they were in neighbouring Essex.

Their major settlement in the region was called *Verulamium*. It was an impor-

tant centre and became a *municipium*, a settlement whose occupants were granted the same rights and privileges as Roman citizens. Some reminders of the Roman period remain; most evident is the Roman theatre. Unique in Britain, it was once a 6000-seater stadium with a stage at one end.

The First Martyr

During the late 2nd and early 3rd centuries AD, early Christianity was beginning to infiltrate Roman Britain but, as in the rest of the Empire, these early Christians were persecuted. In about 209, one such Christian was being sheltered in *Verulamium* by a Roman soldier called Alban. The secret was uncovered and Alban was killed – and became the first Christian martyr in Britain. The spot where he died later became a shrine and, sometime after the Romans withdrew from Britain, the Saxons built an abbey in his memory. The Abbey of St. Alban was founded in the 8th century and – by the 11th century – *Verulamium* had been re-named as St. Albans.

St. Albans Abbey was dissolved in 1539 and all the buildings were destroyed, apart from the Abbey's church which became St. Albans Parish Church and is now St. Albans Cathedral. At 168 m (550 ft) it is one of the longest in the country and is distinctive because much of the structure was built using Roman stones and bricks plundered from the ruins of *Verulamium*.

The Oldest Pub?

St. Albans continued as an important trading and communications centre through the centuries, being conveniently situated near the major trade routes north from London. One sign of this continued significance is the number of inns in the town.

One of these, *The Fighting Cocks*, is a contender for the title of 'Oldest Pub in Britain'. The present building has an 11th-century structure built on top of 8th-century foundations, and it is thought that the building was originally a fishing lodge for the Abbey.

Ducal Piles and Mighty Homes

Due to its pleasant countryside and easy access to London, the region has long been a favourite site for the homes of the rich and famous. Important estates include Knebworth House, Hatfield House, Luton Hoo, Woburn Abbey and Blenheim Palace.

Woburn Abbey, home of the Duke of Bedford, is set within the largest privately-owned park in the country, which covers an area of 1200 ha (3000 acres).

Blenheim Palace

Blenheim Palace, seat of the Duke of Marlborough, was paid for by a grateful nation following the first Duke's (John Churchill) victory over the French, in 1704. It is set in a park of 800 ha (2000 acres).

The Palace was created by Vanbrugh and is a huge baroque building covering a floor space of 2.8 ha (7 acres). Sir Winston Churchill was born there, in 1875, and is buried in the graveyard of the nearby village of Bladon. Blenheim is the third most popular stately home in the country, attracting more than 500 000 paying visitors every year.

Royal Windsor

All the magnificent buildings and great estates of the dukes pale into insignificance when compared to Windsor Castle. It was founded by William the Conqueror as a strategic point to control London and was built on a cliff overlooking the River Thames, roughly one-day's march from the City.

Over the centuries, the Castle has been fortified, re-built and extended by many

Below: St. Alban's Roman theatre.

monarchs and has been a favourite home for many of them.

Henry II built the first stone fortifications in the 1150s and started work on the Round Tower. Other major royal improvers of Windsor include Elizabeth I, Charles II, George IV and Victoria.

Above: Windsor Castle.

The resulting structure presents two faces to the world. Viewed from the river and the town of Windsor, it is an impressive fortress with its curtain walls and central keep (the Round Tower). From Home Park, it presents the spectacular display of a palatial royal residence, with imposing buildings looking out over Long Walk.

Windsor Castle is still a popular royal residence and is the largest inhabited castle in the world and the largest castle in Europe. The curtain walls form a figure-of-eight-style waisted parallelogram measuring 576 m (1890 ft) by 164 m (540 ft), enclosing an area of 5.3 ha (13 acres).

Inside the curtain wall, the Castle neatly divides into three wards. The Lower Ward includes St. George's Chapel. Begun in 1475, it is now regarded as the finest medieval Gothic church in Britain, and is the home church of the Knights of the Order of the Garter. The Middle Ward is dominated by the Round Tower, a circular castle keep

Right: Milton Keynes.

Licensed to Thrill

The area from west London out into the Thames and Chiltern region has long been famous as an area of film studios, with memorable names including Ealing, Elstree, Shepperton, Denham, Beaconsfield and Pinewood.

Sadly, few of these are still active in the movie business, although Elstree produces the TV soap opera EastEnders, and Beaconsfield is the home of the National Film and Television School.

Pinewood Studios, however, continues and is the home of the world's largest studio stage. It was built in 1976 for the James Bond movie The Spy Who Loved Me *and measures 102 m × 42 m × 12 m (336 ft × 139 ft × 41 ft). During filming, it was used to hold 4.54 million litres (1.2 million gallons) of water and full-scale sections of a 600 000 ton oil tanker, as well as three nuclear submarines.*

with views over 11 counties. The Upper Ward contains the State Apartments with collections of paintings and the famous Queen Mary's Doll's House. It also houses the private apartments of the present Royal Family.

The Playing Fields

Across the Thames from Windsor and linked to it by an 1821 bridge is the town of Eton.

Eton College was founded by Henry VI in 1440, and is the most famous public school in Britain, if not the world. It was the Duke of Wellington who commented that, 'the Battle of Waterloo was won on the playing fields of Eton'.

The College's finest and earliest building is the Chapel, which was started in 1441. It is similar to Kings College Chapel, in Cambridge, which was also founded by Henry VI. It contains some of the finest wall paintings in Europe, which were originally painted around 1486, whitewashed over at the time of the Reformation, and only revealed again in the early part of the 20th century.

The stained glass in the Chapel had to be replaced when the originals were damaged by a bomb, in 1940, and the replacements include eight John Piper windows.

A New Town

Milton Keynes was the logical end-product of the decision to create a series of new towns around the fringes of London, as a way of coping with overspill population beyond the capital's 'green belt'.

It was planned as the last and largest of the new towns, with an anticipated end population of around 210 000. By the end of 1991, the population had reached 160 000 and is on target to reach the estimated figure by 2005.

Milton Keynes has attracted 2800 companies, including nearly 300 from out-

Above: Bekonscot, the world's oldest model village.

side Britain, and over £5000 million of private investment. Its £40 million central shopping area contains the longest mall in the world, measuring 650 m (2133 ft).

University Challenge

Milton Keynes is also the home of the Open University. The OU is a unique distance-learning university that relocated to Milton Keynes in 1971 and enables thousands of would-be scholars of all ages and backgrounds to study for degrees in the comfort of their own homes.

Bekonscot

Beaconsfield is the home of the Bekonscot Model Village. Founded in 1929, it is the oldest model village in the world and includes accurate-scale houses, gardens and a railway.

East Anglia

From Churches and Mills to the Oldest Competition

The eastern counties of Cambridgeshire, Norfolk, Suffolk and Essex form the lowest-lying and flattest part of Britain. Holme Fen in Cambridgeshire holds the record as the lowest part of the country at 2.75 m (9 ft) below sea level, and the rest of the Fens are criss-crossed with drainage channels and sluices to control water levels. Understandably, windmills are as much of a feature of the landscape in this region as they are in Holland.

Religion has always played a major part in the life of the rural communities of East Anglia. In addition to cathedrals and the remains of abbeys, every community there built its own place of worship and it is estimated that there are 2000 churches in the region – a greater concentration than in any other area of the country.

The low-lying nature of the land, the openness of the landscape and the constant presence of water create a unique light in the area, particularly in Norfolk and Suffolk. It is this light that has inspired painters over the centuries, notably Constable and Gainsborough.

East Anglia is also the home of a miscellany of superlatives, including castles and seaside piers, and a strange old challenge for married couples.

Cherished Churches

Given the large number of churches in East Anglia and the way the local communities have cared for them over the centuries, it is hardly surprising that the region contains some spectacular ecclesiastical buildings.

St. Andrew's

The most notable of these is probably St. Andrew's Church at Greenstead, in Essex. It is wooden and its walls are made from tree trunks that were split and erected with the rounded outside of the trunks forming the church's outer walls, and the flat, split surfaces forming the inner walls. The timbers have been scientifically dated and reveal that the church was constructed around AD850, making it the oldest wooden church in Britain.

The Round Church

The Church of the Holy Sepulchre in Cambridge is one of only four round churches in Britain, a design inspired by Crusaders returning from the Holy Land. Cambridge's round church was founded in 1130 and is the oldest of its kind in the country.

All Shapes and Sizes

Meanwhile, 13th-century All Saints Church in Maldon, Essex, has the only triangular church tower in Britain.

The Octagonal Tower at Ely Cathedral was erected in 1335 to replace the Central Tower of the original 1083 building. It is the only tower of its type in Britain and its deceptive construction gives the interior of the Cathedral a wonderful open feeling, with the entire Tower supported by only eight arches. Misleading indeed, as the Tower in turn supports a 14th-century wooden lantern and the whole structure weighs more than 400 tons.

Colleges and Chapels

Cambridge University was founded in 1209 by students fleeing from unrest at

Left: Colchester Castle.

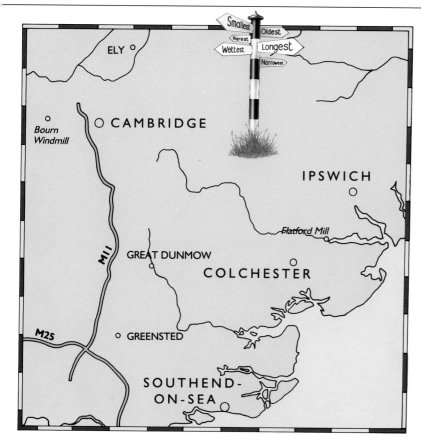

Sutton

Sutton Windmill in Norfolk is the tallest windmill in Britain. It was constructed in 1853, was badly damaged after being struck by lightning in 1941 but has since been restored. The tower has 9 storeys and the windmill sails are 22.2 m (73 ft) in diameter with 216 shutters.

Woodbridge

There is evidence that there has been a tide mill at Woodbridge in Suffolk since the 12th century. The existing wooden clapboard tide mill was constructed in the 18th century and is the oldest working tide mill in the country.

Below: Flatford Mill.

Flatford

The most famous mill in East Anglia is Flatford Mill near East Bergholt in Suffolk. It has no 'claim to fame' in its own right but it is probably the most photographed mill in the world.

John Constable, the famous artist, was born in East Bergholt in 1776, the son

Oxford, Britain's first university. The centre of modern-day Cambridge is dominated by the magnificent buildings erected for the colleges over the centuries. Walking around the streets is undoubtedly the best way to enjoy the town as there are so many architectural delights. Two of the greatest highlights must be Kings College Chapel and Trinity College's Great Court.

King's College

Kings College Chapel is regarded as one of the most notable medieval buildings in Europe. Building was started by Henry VI in 1446, was completed by Henry VIII in 1545 and it has been extended over the centuries. The most recent major alteration was the incorporation of Ruben's *Adoration of the Magi* as the Chapel's altarpiece, in 1971.

The Chapel has enormous windows filled with medieval stained glass allowing light into the huge structure which is 88 m (289 ft) long, 12 m (40 ft) wide and 24 m (80 ft) high.

Trinity College

Trinity College's Great Court is the largest enclosed courtyard in Britain. Built round a 1602 fountain, it is a rectangle measuring 104 m (340 ft) by 88 m (288 ft). The student tradition of racing around Great Court whilst the clock strikes 12 o'clock noon was immortalised in the 1981 film *Chariots of Fire*.

Milling Around

East Anglia was once covered by hundreds of mills, some used for drainage and some for flour production. Thanks to the actions of various preservation groups, many can still be found in working condition.

Bourn

The windmill at Bourn in Cambridgeshire is a post mill – that is to say that the whole structure revolves around a central support. It is not certain exactly when it was built but there is proof that it was in use in 1636, and it is the oldest surviving mill in Britain.

Opposite: Bourn Mill, the oldest surviving mill in Britain.

of the successful corn merchant who owned the mill. Instead of following in his father's footsteps, however, Constable decided to paint the *Haywain* which immortalised Flatford Mill on canvas. Now a National Trust property, the mill has been preserved so that Constable's inspiration can be recaptured by modern artists and photographers.

Colchester

Colchester lays claim to being the oldest town in Britain and it certainly has some impressive credentials.

Roman Relics

Cunobelin became the King of this part of England in AD10 and built his capital there. The Romans invaded in AD43, destroyed Cunobelin's town and built a settlement. In AD60, Boadicea razed the settlement as part of her Iceni Revolt, but the Romans quickly defeated her and re-built Colchester as a walled and fortified town. The massive Balkerne Gate is the largest Roman relic in the town and the remains of the temple can be seen under the castle keep.

Castle Keep

The keep is all that remains of the Castle built by the Normans around 1075, but

Above: The church, Greenstead.

it is the largest keep in the whole of Europe. The structure is a rectangle measuring 46.3 m (152 ft) by 33.5 m (110 ft), with walls 27.5 m (90 ft) high (rising to 33.5 m (110 ft) at the corner towers) and 3.8 m (12½ ft) thick.

Southend

Southend-on-Sea began to be developed as a seaside resort at the end of the 18th century. It received its name because it was a purpose-built development at the south end of the village of Prittlewell. It was designed to attract daytrippers from London arriving by steamer and latterly by train.

The Longest Pier

All the normal seaside-town attractions of promenades, amusements and gardens can be found in Southend but its crowning glory is the pier, which was originally built in 1890 and extended in 1930. It is 2158 m (7080 ft) long and is the longest seaside pier in the world. For the lethargic tourist there is a narrow-gauge railway running from the pierhead to its end.

The Dunmow Flitch

The Dunmow Flitch is a strange competition held in the village of Great Dunmow, in Essex, every Whit Monday. A 'flitch' is a whole side of pork, and married couples can nominate themselves to receive the award providing that they can convince a jury of the truth of the following statement:

'Having been married for at least a year and a day, we have never once, sleeping or waking, regretted our marriage or wished ourselves single again.'

Centuries ago, when the flitch was awarded by the Lord of the Manor, the ceremony was considered a serious event. However, because a whole side of pork was an expensive prize, a number of lords tried to have the competition banned. They did not succeed and now the flitch is awarded by the town. Evidence suggests that it was first presented in 1244, making it the oldest recorded competition (for 'ordinary' people) in the country.

The Heart of England

Birds, Bridges and the Bard

The Heart of England stretches from the Welsh borders to Oxfordshire and from the Peak District to the Cotswolds. It includes some beautiful landscapes, particularly in the Cotswolds, the Malvern Hills and the Welsh Marches. Many rivers flow through the region, including Britain's longest, the Severn. It rises in Powys, in Wales, and flows for 354 km (220 miles) before entering the Bristol Channel through the Severn Estuary and, for most of this length, it is within the Heart of England. The valley of the Severn and its many tributaries, including the Wye, offer delightful countryside and habitats for wildlife. Overlooking the Severn at Slimbridge is the home of Sir Peter Scott's Wildfowl and Wetlands Trust.

But the story of the region is also very much the story of its towns. These include historic Warwick and Stratford, the three cathedral cities of Gloucester, Hereford and Worcester and the industrial centres of Birmingham, Coventry and Telford.

The Heart of England is also the home of Alton Towers, the largest and most popular theme park in Britain.

Best of the Birds

Slimbridge in Gloucestershire was the first centre to be established by the Wildfowl & Wetlands Trust, when it was set up by Sir Peter Scott, in 1946. The Centre has a resident collection of wildfowl housed in 38 ha (94 acres) of ground and a refuge for migrating wildfowl that covers another 323 ha (800 acres).

Slimbridge is host to around 3300 birds representing 164 different species and sub-species. The collection includes 400 flamingos and this is the only place in Britain with representatives of all six types of flamingo. It is the world's largest and most varied wildfowl centre and attracts around 245 000 visitors per year.

Thousands of Trees

Upon the Cotswolds, near Tetbury, is the Westonbirt Arboretum. It was founded in 1829 by Robert Holford and, since 1956, it has been owned and run by the Forestry Commission. Its collection of temperate trees and shrubs is the best in Britain and one of the most noteworthy in the world, and even includes Giant Redwoods.

The 14 000 trees and shrubs in the Arboretum are planted in an area of 200 ha (500 acres) of woodland and 40 ha (100 acres) of downland; the area is crossed by 27 km (17 miles) of paths for ease of access.

Warwick Castle

Warwick Castle is one of the most spectacular and forbidding castles in Britain, particularly when viewed from the River Avon where the walls and towers appear to soar straight into the sky.

William the Conqueror founded a Norman castle on the sandstone bluff overlooking the river in 1068, replacing a Saxon fortification built around

Left: Westonbirt.

Above: Warwick Castle.

913. The present castle is, however, mainly 14th-century, the work of the Beauchamp family.

Two Towers

Guy Beauchamp (aka 'The Black Dog of Arden') is commemorated in Guy's Tower, one of the castle's great defensive positions. The mighty Caesar's Tower complements Guy's and dominates the gateway and barbican.

Stately Home

Over the centuries, Warwick functioned as much as a great baronial home as a fortress and extensive state rooms and halls were created, mainly by the Greville family.

This combination of fortress and stately home makes Warwick Castle a very popular tourist attraction. It is the most popular stately home in Britain and, in 1990, it was visited by 685 000 people.

The Bard

Stratford-upon-Avon is synonymous with William Shakespeare. Indeed, the entire business activity of Stratford often seems to be focused entirely on Shakespeare.

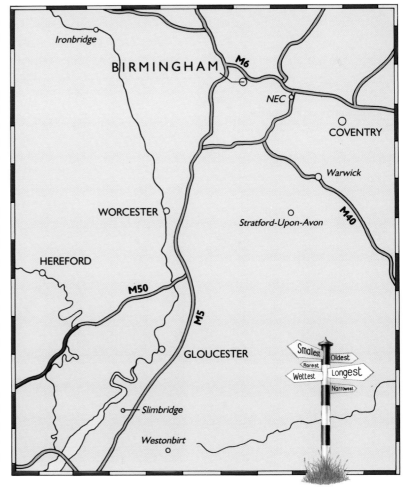

Below: Shakespeare's Monument.

The greatest poet and playwright in English history was born in the town on 23 April, 1564, or in any event, that is the day the town celebrates his birthday every year. His works were mostly performed in the famous Elizabethan theatres of Southwark, in London, but Stratford and the surrounding area is full of memories of the Bard and, of course, the town is the home of the Royal Shakespeare Company and the Royal Shakespeare Theatre.

These attractions pull in more than 500 000 visitors a year and in between theatre performances they can visit: Shakespeare's birthplace, Anne Hathaway's Cottage, Mary Arden's House, New Place/Nash's House, Hall's Croft and Holy Trinity Church (where Will is buried).

Three Choirs

There are three great medieval cathedrals in the southwest of the region – Gloucester, Hereford and Worcester. All three are well worth visiting and are linked by a memorable festival.

Gloucester

Gloucester Cathedral has the largest single stained glass window in Britain. It was made in 1350 to commemorate the

Opposite: Gloucester Cathedral contains Britain's largest single stained glass window.

Battle of Crècy and measures 21.94 m (72 ft) by 11.58 m (38 ft).

Hereford

Hereford Cathedral is the home of the largest chained library in the world. It contains 1440 books, including 8th-century illuminated Gospels, which are housed in 17th-century bookcases.

Thunderlooper

Travel 22.5 km (14 miles) east of Stoke-on-Trent and you can enter a different world altogether, Alton Towers.

Alton Towers Theme Park stands on the former Alton Towers estate of the Earls of Shrewsbury. The gardens and waterworks were created in the early 19th century by the 15th Earl. In 1860, the 18th Earl opened the gardens to the public for the first time and it is recorded that, in that year, the income from gate receipts was £116. 17s. 5d (£116.87). By the 1890s, crowds of 30 000 were flocking there to watch displays of acrobats and the bravery of lion tamers.

In 1924, the estate was sold to a group of local businessmen, but the true story of Alton Towers in the 20th century really started in 1942 with Dennis Bagshaw, continued with John Broome (his son-in-law), and goes on today with the Tussards Group, who took control in 1990.

Alton Towers has developed into the largest and most popular theme park in Britain and is currently rated amongst the top five theme parks in the world. In 1990, it attracted 2 070 000 paying visitors. The 81 ha (200 acre) site has more than 125 rides and attractions, over a third of which are indoors, and one of the restaurants, the Talbot, is the biggest fast food restaurant in Britain, serving 2000 guests an hour.

Thunderlooper, by the way, is the name of Britain's largest single loop rollercoaster, whose home is Alton Towers.

THE GUINNESS BOOK OF BRITAIN

Hereford also possesses the *Mappa Mundi*, a unique medieval map of the then known world, centred on Jerusalem. Drawn on vellum, it was created by Richard di Bello, in 1289.

Below: The Mappa Mundi.

Worcester Cathedral is the resting place of King John, who died in 1216. His tomb is made of Purbeck marble and was erected in 1232. It is surmounted by an effigy of the King which was created in 1218, making it the oldest surviving royal effigy in Britain.

Three Choirs

The event that links the three cathedrals is the Three Choirs Festival. Musical tradition within the area is very strong and the cathedrals combine every year to hold a major festival, alternating each year between the three cities. The Three Choirs Festival was first held in 1724 and is the oldest music festival in Britain.

The Darby Family

During the 18th century, a new type of powerful 'baron' developed – the Ironmaster. Amongst the greatest and most significant were Abraham Darby and his family.

Just to the south of the town of Telford, a new town named after Thomas Telford the great Victorian engineer, the River Severn flows through a gorge called Coalbrookdale. If any place in the world deserves the label 'cradle of the Industrial Revolution' it is this place.

It was here, in 1709, that Abraham Darby first succeeded in smelting iron

Below: The bridge at Ironbridge.

using coke rather than charcoal, a process which suddenly made the mass production of iron possible and affordable. In 1758, his son, Abraham Darby Jr, founded the world's first commercial blast furnace based on his father's techniques.

Ironbridge

Twenty-one years later, Abraham Darby III, the grandson, built the world's first iron bridge at the place in Coalbrookdale that is now known as Ironbridge. The bridge still stands spanning what is now called Ironbridge Gorge. It is 30 m (100 ft) long and rises 18 m (45 ft) to the highest point of its arch. Although made totally of iron, it was built using the principles of wooden bridge construction, using no bolts. All of the individual sections of iron were cast to fit together using 'carpentry-style' joints.

Coalbrookdale and Ironbridge are also the location where Richard Trevithick constructed the world's first steam-powered locomotive, and the whole area is full of remains and re-constructions of the beginnings of the modern world.

Coventry

Coventry was already established as a Saxon town when Leofric, Earl of Mercia, undertook its development in the 11th century. Over the centuries, it became rich and powerful – initially through wool and latterly through precision engineering.

Destruction and Re-birth

St. Michael's Church, with its superb spire, was built from the 14th century onwards and became a cathedral at the start of the 20th century. Then, on the night of 14 November, 1940, the heart of the city was destroyed and St. Michael's devastated in a single blitz by massed German bomber aircraft.

After the War, Coventry was re-built and a new cathedral rose from the ashes. Sir Basil Spence created the award-winning design and produced an un-

Above: Coventry Cathedral – uncompromisingly modern.

compromisingly modern Cathedral to sit alongside the ruins of St. Michael's, with the two physically linked to show continuity.

The new building was completed in 1962 and it contains some spectacular modern works of religious art. These include Epstein's sculpture, *St. Michael and the Devil,* and John Piper's magnificent Baptistry Window. The crowning glory is, however, *Christ in his Majesty*, a tapestry created by Graham Sutherland. In addition to being fascinating, it is 23 m (75 ft) tall, the tallest tapestry in Britain.

NEC

Just to the southeast of Birmingham is what is, in effect, a mini-city in its own right. The complex includes Birmingham International Airport and Birmingham International Railway Station, but the focus of the development is the National Exhibition Centre.

The NEC was opened in 1976 and it is the largest exhibition and conference centre in Britain and the tenth largest in the world. Covering 250 ha (600 acres), the total capacity of the halls is currently 125 000 m² (1 345 000 sq. ft).

South Wales

Countryside and Castles, Bridges and Tunnels

South Wales is often catalogued as a heavy industrial area full of coal mines and steelworks. The truth is rather different – the region has its industries but it also contains the Brecon Beacons and the Pembrokeshire Coast, two of Wales' three National Parks. Additionally, the Gower Peninsular was, in 1956, the first area of Britain to be designated An Area of Outstanding Natural Beauty.

South Wales was an important centre for the Romans, not least because Welsh goldmines were a vast source of assets for the Imperial treasury. Caerleon and Caerwent are the most important Roman remains in Wales, and are amongst the most important in Britain.

Almost every town of any size in the region has the remains of its castle. Chepstow's was the first stone castle in the country and Caerphilly's is the largest in Wales, second only to Windsor in the British Isles.

Religion has played a vital role in the region since St. David arrived in the 6th century, and the cathedrals at St. David's and Llandaff give clear evidence of this importance.

One of the area's problems over the centuries has been its relative isolation from England. The south and east of the region look over towards the English West Country, but the mighty River Severn and its estuary forms a major obstacle. Until 1966, the lowest road-crossing point was at Gloucester, 98 km (61 miles) northeast of Cardiff.

Fishguard, in the west of the region, has a unique claim to fame as the location of the last armed invasion of the British mainland, and Wales' oldest inn, the Skirrid Inn, still shows how justice used to be dispensed.

Parks

The Pembrokeshire Coast National Park is the smallest National Park in Britain and the only one to be based on a coastline. It was created in 1952 and covers only 583 km² (225 sq. miles) but is 288 km (180 miles) long, stretching roughly from Tenby in the south round the coast almost to Cardigan in the north. It rarely extends more than a few kilometres inland, except in the north where it bulges to encompass the Preseli Hills, the Park's highest point at 536 m (1760 ft).

Brecon Beacons

The Brecon Beacons National Park is the most recent National Park to be created, having been designated in 1967. It has an area of 1344 km² (519 sq. miles) and covers a number of mountain ranges forming a northern barrier to the region. From east to west, the ranges are the Black Mountains, the Brecon Beacons and, confusingly, the Black Mountain. The Park's highest point is Pen y Fan in the Brecon Beacons, which reaches 886 m (2907 ft).

Roman Centres

The Romans established their bases in Wales about 30 years after their invasion of Britain. Because of the need to control the Silures and other Welsh tribes, and their need to protect their valuable mining interests, one of the major legionary fortresses was built in the region.

Below: Roman remains, Caerleon.

Caerleon

Caerleon was known to the Romans as *Isca* and was founded in AD75. It was the only legionary fort in Wales, housed the famous 2nd Legion and ranked alongside Chester and York as Roman military centres. It was made famous during Sir Mortimer Wheeler's excavations in the 1920s, and the uncovered remains include Wales' largest Roman amphitheatre and barrack blocks.

Caerwent

Nearby Caerwent was the largest Roman civilian town in Wales. It was founded at the same time as Caerleon and housed around 2000 people in a sophisticated walled town covering 17 ha (44 acres). The remains of the walls and some of the villas are clearly visible today.

Two Cathedrals

St. David's

St. David's is a village in the far west of South Wales – it is dominated by St. David's Cathedral and the remains of St. David's Bishop's Palace. The presence of the Cathedral makes St. David's officially a city and, with a population of only 2000, it is the smallest cathedral city in Britain and reputedly the smallest in the world. Building of the current Cathedral was started in 1176 but the site has been a world-famous religious centre since St. David founded his monastery there in the 6th century.

Llandaff

Cardiff, the capital city of Wales, is the site of a Roman fort built in AD75, but

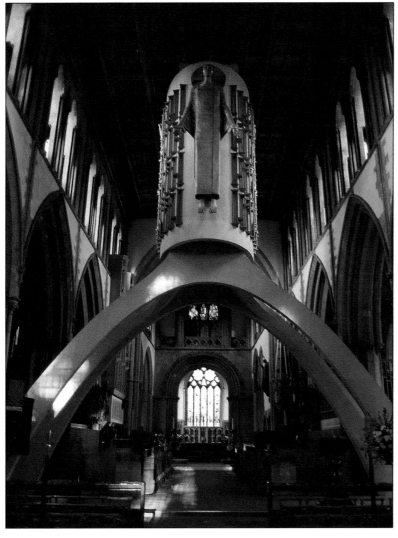

Above: Llandaff Cathedral.

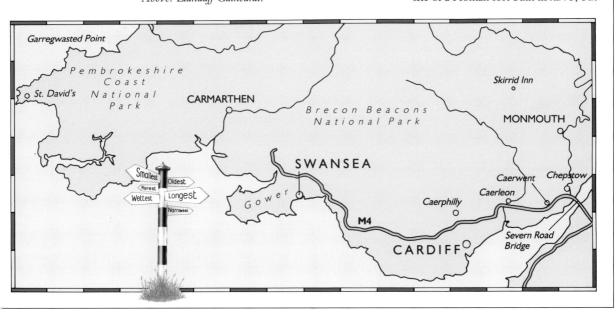

the city was only named as the official capital of Wales in 1955. Its complex of civic buildings were built in Cathay Park by the Marquess of Bute between 1905 and 1938 and it is regarded as the finest civic centre in Britain.

Two miles west of the Civic Centre, in a Cardiff suburb, is Llandaff Cathedral.

Llandaff's story is often regarded as one of the greatest examples of religion triumphing over adversity. The present building was erected in 1120 and was an important religious and cultural centre in medieval Britain. During the Civil War, it was stripped and Cromwell's soldiers used it as an alehouse. It was subsequently allowed to fall into disre-

Above: St. David's Cathedral.

pair for nearly 200 years, until it was refurbished and returned to its former glory between 1835 and 1869.

In 1941, at the height of the Second World War, it was the victim of a direct hit from a German landmine and the interior was very badly damaged. However, restoration was completed in the 1950s and the Cathedral re-opened in 1957. The crowning glory of the new interior is a huge concrete parabolic arch soaring over the nave. This supports a hollow cylinder housing the Cathedral's organworks, and on the cylinder is mounted Sir Jacob Epstein's magnificent aluminium statue, *Christ in Majesty*.

Fortifications

Chepstow Castle

Chepstow Castle was founded on a bluff overlooking the town and the Severn by William FitzOsbern in 1067. Unusually, and presumably because its position on the bluff precluded the traditional early Norman timber motte and bailey design, it was constructed from the start in stone. Work on the central stone tower commenced in 1068 and it is the oldest of its kind in Britain. It is a rectangle 30 m (100 ft) by 12 m (40 ft) and was originally two storeys high, until a third was added in the 13th century.

Caerphilly Castle

Building work on Caerphilly Castle started in 1268 and it was the first purpose-built concentric castle in Britain. The rings of defences are formidable – the outer curtain wall has a circumference of 290 m (960 ft) and is surrounded by an extensive network of defensive moats and lakes. The total area of land and water fortifications is 12 ha (30 acres), making Caerphilly the largest castle in Wales.

During the Civil War, Cromwell's forces tried to 'slight' the Castle to make it indefensible. Their explosions succeeded in undermining the foundations of the South East Tower, but all that happened was that the tower tilted. It is still standing and leans at a greater angle than the world-famous Leaning Tower of Pisa.

Monnow Bridge

South Wales' most unusual fortification is on the Monnow Bridge in

Hanging About in Bars

The Skirrid Mountain Inn, northwest of Monmouth, is the oldest inn in Wales and one of the oldest in Britain, dating from 1110. It used to serve as the local courthouse . . . and place of execution.

The Skirrid has an unusual square spiral staircase, said to be the only one in Britain, with a large open well from floor to ceiling surrounded by the staircase. Condemned prisoners were taken to the top of the staircase and hung down the well. Over the centuries, it is thought that approximately 1000 people were put to death in this way, although it is reported that the current landlord treats the Inn's customers much better!

Above: Monnow Bridge.

Opposite: The Severn Bridge.

Monmouth. The centre of the bridge is surmounted by a huge 13th-century fortified tower gateway. It was part of Monmouth's medieval town defences and is the only fortified bridge still standing in Britain.

Bridging the Gap

The Severn Estuary was an impressive barrier to trade. The waters of Britain's longest river pour downstream and the funnel-like nature of the estuary causes strong currents, eddies and the famous Severn Bore. It was an uncrossable barrier until the 19th century but, of course, it could not stop the pioneering Victorians. It was beyond their technology to bridge the gap, but they could tunnel under it. Naturally, given the Age, it was a rail tunnel and it was excavated between 1873 and 1886. The work of Sir John Hawkshaw, it was opened on 1 September, 1886. Its total length is 7.01 km (4 miles, 1884 ft) and it is lined with 76 400 000 bricks. Until the Channel Tunnel opens, it will continue to be the longest mainline rail tunnel in Britain.

Suspension Bridge

The planning of the M4 motorway to link London, Bristol, Cardiff and Swan-sea meant that the road would also have to cross the estuary. The 20th-century engineers decided to bridge it and chose Chepstow as the Welsh end of the bridge.

The suspension bridge they built opened in 1966 and is 988 m (3241 ft) long, making it the longest road suspension bridge in Wales, the third longest in Britain and the ninth longest in the world.

Invasion

Carregwastad Point, near Fishguard, has a place in history as the location of the last military invasion of Britain, although the invasion only lasted two days.

On 22 February, 1797, an Irish American, General William Tate, led ashore a force of 1200 French soldiers to challenge the might of George III. They were met by a small force of local troops and townspeople and the invading forces surrendered on 24 February. Local legend has it that they surrendered because the local women were all wearing the traditional Welsh costume and, from a distance, the French invaders thought they were being surrounded by crack British Redcoats!

Below: Fishguard.

Mid Wales

From Ancient Fortifications to the Victorian Seaside

Above: Powis Castle.

Mid Wales is often ignored, or overshadowed, by the more obvious attractions of the north and south of the Principality, but the area contains much of fascination, including some of the best-preserved sections of Offa's Dyke, the great earthwork that marked the boundary between Wales and Mercia in the 8th century.

Machynlleth was Owain Glyndwr's capital in the 1400s and Powis Castle at Welshpool was the stronghold of the Princes of Powys.

Aberystwyth is one of Wales' most popular seaside resorts. Developed by the Victorians, it is also a university and administrative centre, and the terminal of the Vale of Rheidol Railway. At the other end of the railway is Devil's Bridge with its unique collection of three bridges above one another and some spectacular waterfalls.

Whilst on the subject of water, Mid Wales also has a number of valleys that have been flooded to hold water for Liverpool and Birmingham. The construction of the dams for these reservoirs has created some exceptional civil engineering achievements.

Finally, Welshpool is not only famous because of Powis Castle, it is also the only place in the country where a complete cockpit has been preserved intact from the days before the horrendous 'sport' was banned.

Offa's Dyke

Offa was probably the greatest of the Kings of Mercia. He ruled between AD750 and 800, was acknowledged and respected on the Continent and left a lasting legacy.

Offa's Dyke is an earthwork formed of a complex of banks up to 8 m (25 ft) high and ditches up to 4.5 m (15 ft) deep. It was constructed around 784 and stretches 270 km (168 miles) from the River Wye to the North Wales coast. It is not a continuous barrier because – in Offa's day – there were impenetrable forests and other natural obstacles along the route, and where these existed the dyke was not needed. It was not manned in the same way as Hadrian's Wall but was intended as a physical deterrent and warning to marauding Welsh tribes.

Offa's Dyke is the greatest remaining earthwork of the Dark Ages in Britain and some of the best-preserved sections are around Knighton in Mid Wales.

Powis Castle

The present Powis Castle was built around 1300, although there are remains of an earlier Norman structure. It was damaged during the Civil War and was repaired from 1667 onwards by the Herbert family. It was inherited by the family of Clive of India, and the Castle

Left: The dam, Llyn Brianne.

*Devil's Bridge, where the waters of
the Mynach join the Rheidol.*

Above: Devil's Bridge Falls.

contains numerous relics from Clive and his son's time on the sub-continent.

Gardens

It is, however, the gardens at Powis Castle that make the place famous. The formal gardens were laid out between 1688 and 1720 and consist of four hanging terraces, each 180 m (600 ft) long, with lead statues dotted amongst the vegetation. They are the oldest gardens of their type to survive in Britain without being altered by subsequent landscape gardeners.

Owain Glyndwr

Owain Glyndwr was the last native-born Prince of Wales. At the end of the 14th century he was a powerful nobleman who had fought for the English cause in Scotland, but Henry IV's disposal of Richard II turned him into a rebel. He fought the English King from 1400 to 1412, captured many castles – including Harlech – and united Wales. In 1404, he held a parliament at Machynlleth and proclaimed himself Prince of Wales.

Below: Parliament House.

The site of the last native Welsh parliament is reputedly where the present Parliament House and Owain Glyndwr Centre is (in the centre of Machynlleth), although the building occupying the site was not constructed until the end of the 15th century.

St. Stephen's

St. Stephen's Church in Old Radnor is a 14th-century building containing two remarkable antiques. The font is carved out of a huge glacial boulder that reputedly was used as an altar stone for pagan

Cockfighting

Cockfighting (and the gambling associated with it) was a very popular 'sport' in the Middle Ages and was not made illegal until 1849.

In the early 1700s, Welshpool acquired a new, spectacular six-sided cockpit and it continued to be a popular venue until the fighting was outlawed. Remarkably, the entire building has been preserved on its original site and has been restored. It is the only such specimen in Wales.

Above: Lake Vyrnwy.

rituals during the Bronze Age. The Church also possesses a fine linen organ case – dated at around 1500, it is the oldest in Britain.

Seaside and Scholars

Around Aberystwyth there are remains of settlements from the Iron Age onwards and the town has had a castle since around 1100, but the success and prosperity of the town really dates from Victorian times and the arrival of the railway.

The town is overlooked by Constitution Hill and, in 1896, the Aberystwyth Electric Cliff Railway was constructed to allow holidaymakers to travel the 130 m (430 ft) to the summit. At the top of the Hill is the world's biggest Camera Obscura which reflects the view over 96 km (60 miles) of Welsh landscape.

Endless Books

The first constituent college of what was to become the University of Wales opened in the town in 1872, and the National Library of Wales was located

in the town at the start of the 20th century. The Library has a collection of more than 2 000 000 books, including many precious early Welsh-language volumes, the greatest of which is *The Black Book of Carmarthen*. Dating from the 12th century, it is the oldest book in Welsh.

Three Bridges

One of Wales' little trains, the Vale of Rheidol Railway, runs from Aberystwyth for 19 km (12 miles) inland to Devil's Bridge. The fast-flowing River Rheidol and River Mynach meet there and the water is spanned by three bridges, built one above another. The top bridge is an iron structure built in 1901; the middle a stone bridge from 1753, and the bottom bridge, also of stone, was reputedly built in 1087 by monks from Strata Florida Abbey. In spite of this, the Welsh name for it means literally 'bridge of the evil one', and legend has it that it was created by the devil in an unsuccessful bid to ensnare the soul of a woman who needed to cross the water.

At Devil's Bridge the waters of the Mynach fall 120 m (400 ft) to join the Rheidol, creating a spectacular series of waterfalls and cascades.

Drinking Water

Of the many reservoirs in Mid Wales the most famous are: Lake Vyrnwy, the Elan Valley Reservoirs, the Claerwen Reservoir and Llyn Brianne.

Vyrnwy
The dam at Vyrnwy is 355 m (1170 ft) long and 44 m (144 ft) high. It was completed in 1881 – the resulting lake has an area of 8.2 km² (3.18 sq. miles) and is the largest lake in Wales.

Elan and Llyn Brianne
The Elan Valley Reservoirs were built between 1892 and 1896, and Claerwen in 1952. Llyn Brianne is the most recent, having been completed in November 1971. It is also the most impressive as, with a height of 91 m (298½ ft), it is the tallest dam in Britain.

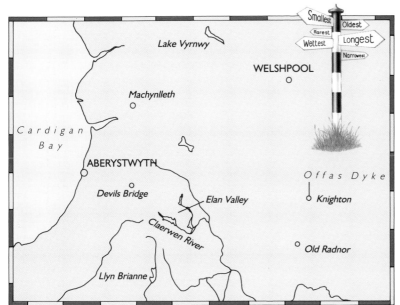

North Wales

Mountains and Rivers, Engineers and Holidaymakers

It is no wonder that the mountains of North Wales provided the Welsh with their last stronghold against the English. They are the highest in the country and the rivers pour down from them in torrents that cut through the land. Edward I could only encircle the mountains with his 'ring of iron' castles, and it took the incomparable talents of two of Victoria's finest engineers to tame the landscape and open up the country.

After they succeeded, North Wales was finally conquered by Victorian gentry taking a 'tour' and by holidaymakers and daytrippers in the 20th century.

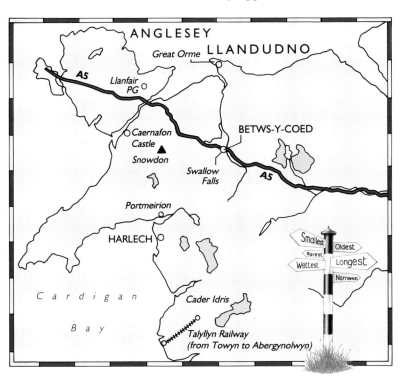

Snowdonia

Even on the coast or the island of Anglesey the mountains of Snowdonia catch the eye and capture one's imagination. They are rugged, beautiful and full of mystery.

Snowdonia National Park

The Snowdonia National Park was created in 1951. It covers 2170 km² (838 sq. miles) and is the largest park in Wales. More importantly, Snowdonia is not just one mountain. The Park contains 14 separate peaks over 900 m

(2950 ft) and they are the 14 highest summits in the whole of Wales.

When you add to these statistics the brooding mass of Cader Idris on the southern edge of the Park, you can understand why the mountains are so important. Cader Idris is only 892 m (2927 ft) high but it dominates the Dyfi and Mawddach estuaries.

The highest peak in Snowdonia is Snowdon (or *Yr Wyddfa* in Welsh). It stands 1085 m (3560 ft) high on the northwest edge of the Park and is the highest mountain in Wales. Yet, nearly 250 000 people reach the summit of Snowdon every year – how? In spite of its height, Snowdon is the easiest of the Welsh mountains to scale, thanks to Victorian engineering skill and determination.

The Snowdonia Mountain Railway, built in 1896 with an unusual 2 ft 7½ in gauge, runs from Llanberis to within a few metres walk from the summit of Snowdon, a distance of 8 km (5 miles) during which it climbs 900 m (2950 ft). It takes about an hour to make the journey.

The Railway is unique in Britain as it is the only rack and pinion railway. Each locomotive has a large cog wheel that grips a toothed rail on the track to stop the train sliding down the mountain.

Betws-y-Coed

Betws-y-Coed is probably the best-known village in Wales, although not many people can pronounce its name properly! It is famous because of its water – and the Victorians.

Telford's Turnpike

Three of Snowdonia's rushing mountain rivers meet at Betws-y-Coed – the Conwy, Llugwy and Lledr. As they tumble out of the mountains into the valley, they create some spectacular waterfalls, in particular the Swallow Falls.

The area was hard to get to until Thomas Telford and his fellow engineers began building turnpikes and railways. Telford's great London to Holyhead Turnpike (now the A5) runs through Betws-y-Coed and once it was opened the Victorians arrived to see the amazing sights of nature.

We are still in awe of nature; in 1991, Swallow Falls on the Llugwy was the third most popular natural tourist attraction in Wales and the most-visited waterfall in the whole country, with a total of 261 783 tourists.

Edward I – the First Tourist?

In the middle of the 13th century, Edward I, King of England, decided it was time to bring the Welsh to heel and fought and defeated the armies of Llewelyn.

The defeated Welsh armies retreated into the mountains of Snowdonia to re-group. Edward knew his army could not follow them – the mountains were Welsh territory with the risk of ambush and attack around every corner, but he also knew that if he did nothing, within a decade he would have to challenge them all over again.

So instead he built a 'ring of iron' round the mountains to contain the native tribes. He created a series of mighty fortresses and walled towns to surround and control them. His master builder was James of St. George and it is a tribute to his skill and Edward's determination that the castles they built 700 years ago still exist and remain awe-inspiring: Harlech, Flint, Denbigh, Beaumaris, Conwy and, above all, Caernarfon.

Caernafon Castle

Caernarfon Castle is different from all Edward I's others. It was the largest one to be completed – a mighty fortress with walls 3 m (9 ft) thick and towers 40 m (125 ft) tall. However, it was also designed as a palace and the town enclosed by its walls was to be a royal town.

Right: Betws-y-Coed.

'Prisoner' in Portmeirion

Portmeirion is on a wooded peninsula on the Welsh coast, sandwiched between Porthmadog and Harlech. It is a classic Italian village 'uprooted' from Tuscany. Fans of The Prisoner will tell you that it is 'The Village'.

Portmeirion was the dream of the Welsh designer Sir Clough Williams-Ellis. He planned it in the late 1920s and it was built slowly through the 30s, 50s and 60s.

It is a paradise and one that people can enjoy. In 1991 it attracted over 285 461 visitors and indeed, there is nowhere quite like Portmeirion.

Work began on Caernarfon Castle in 1283 and Edward's son (later Edward II) was born there in 1284, and proclaimed Prince of Wales in 1301. The tradition continued in 1969, when Elizabeth II invested Charles, Prince of Wales, in the castle grounds.

Caernarfon Castle is now a World Heritage Site and in 1990 it attracted 282 000 visitors.

Telford and Stephenson

The Victorian era was the Age of the Engineer and two of the greatest were Thomas Telford and Robert Stephenson. North Wales is fortunate as both created masterpieces there – Telford built his roads and Stephenson the railways.

The dream was to link London with the ferry terminal at Holyhead on the north-west coast of Anglesey. A direct route would cut through the mountains; a more straightforward but longer route following the North Wales coast would have to cross the Conwy estuary, and either route would have to intersect the treacherous Menai Strait which separates Anglesey from the mainland.

Both routes were built with Telford bridging the Strait first, in 1826. He decided to build the world's first sus-pension bridge. The bridge is 386 m (1265 ft) long with a centre span of 54 m (176 ft) and, 166 years on, it continues to carry road traffic over the Menai Strait.

Stephenson built his railway bridge (the first tubular bridge in Britain) in 1850. His construction techniques were so good and the bridge so sound that 20th-century engineers have added a second deck to the original, and the Britannia Tubular Bridge now carries both the Holyhead railway and the A5 over the Menai Strait.

The Talyllyn Railway

Wales is famous for its 'great little trains' and one in particular, in North Wales, is full of superlatives.

The Talyllyn Railway runs for 11 km (7 miles) from Tywyn on the coast at the mouth of the Dyfi to Abergynolwyn in the mountains. It was built in 1865 to carry slate from Abergynolwyn to the coast and it has been in continuous service ever since, the British record for a small railway. When it was threatened with closure in 1951, it became the first of the small railways in Britain to be preserved by a band of volunteer enthusiasts.

Two of its working locomotives are originals, built for the opening of the line in 1865, as are some of its coaches which are the oldest passenger coaches in regular service in the world.

Tourists

At the end of the 19th century, the slate and mining industries in North Wales began to decline as the new forms of transport killed off the network of small working ports. Forward-thinking Welshmen recognised that the new accessibility could be used to create a new industry – tourism. They approached this in a number of different ways . . . With the completion of the London to Holyhead railway, one enterprising Anglesey tradesman realised that visi-

LLANFAIRPWLLGWYNGYLLGOGERYCHWYRNDROBWYLL-LLANTYSILIOGOGOGOCH
RAILWAY STATION

ON SALE HERE
THE
LARGEST
PLATFORM
TICKET
IN THE
WORLD
PRICE ?

tors would want to break up their long rail journeys. There was a station on the line in his town, just north of the Menai Strait crossing, and all the station needed was a good name. So he gave it one: LLANFAIRPWLLGWYNGYLLGO-GERYCHWYRNDROBWLLLLAN-TYSILIOGOGOGOCH.

Literally translated it means 'St. Mary's Church in the hollow of the white hazel, near a rapid whirlpool and the Church of St. Tysilio, near the red cave', but most people just call it LlanfairPG. Since the name was created, it has stood as the longest place name in Britain and as a hook for tourists it certainly worked. People got

off the train to see both the station and the town, and the hundreds of thousands of platform tickets that have been sold in the past 100 years show how successful it has been.

Llandudno

In the 1840s and 50s the mining industry in the town of Llandudno was disappearing. The local landowners, the Mostyns, realised the need to develop a new industry for the town. They planned and created a Victorian seaside town to attract the city-dwellers of Lancashire and the Midlands. They planned so well that today Llandudno is the largest resort in Wales.

The Mostyn's successors are still plan-

Above: The station at LlanfairPG.

ning Llandudno. One of the town's features is Great Orme, a 207 m (678 ft) rock forming the western edge of the town and giving wonderful views over Snowdonia. It is a long walk to the top so, in 1902, the Great Orme Tramway was opened – a 3 ft 6 in gauge double tramway similar to those in San Francisco – it was a sensation in its day.

The Tramway still operates, but nowadays another way to get to the top of Great Orme is on the Llandudno Chairlift, Britain's longest cable car which travels through the air for 1622 m (5320 ft) to take you to the top.

North West England

From the Roman Conquest to Coronation Street

The North West of England is a distinct and distinctive part of the country, surrounded by mountains (Snowdonia to the west, the Pennines to the east and the Lake District to the north) and facing west towards Ireland and America it contains two vibrant industrial cities in Manchester and Liverpool; Blackpool, one of the world's great holiday towns; Chester, a city offering some of the country's greatest Roman and medieval attractions; and much more besides. Some of the greatest Victorian and 20th century engineers and builders have worked in the region and innovations continue to this day.

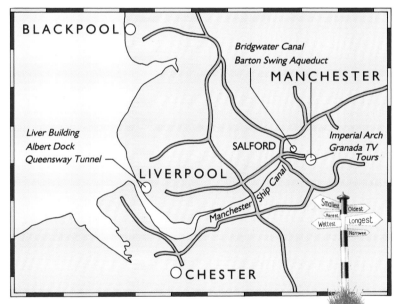

man remains include part of the Quay Walls of the Roman harbour at the Roodee, a 5 m (16 ft) high section of the fortress wall by the present North Gate, and many columns, buttresses and tombstones.

Chester

The Romans left but Deva did not die – it became Chester. There is some evidence that the Roman fortress was never deserted, just taken over by the Welsh tribes and then fought over for centuries until the Norman Conquest when it was finally destroyed.

However, the site was too good to leave and Hugh Lupus, William the Conqueror's nephew who was known as 'The Wolf', was made Earl of Chester and re-built the city. 'The Wolf' was a Norman battlelord and built a fortified town with a mighty castle, little of which remains, but the walls of Chester are the most completely preserved city walls in England. The present walls were completed between the 12th and 14th centuries and have a circumference of 3.2 km (2 miles).

Below: The Rows, Chester.

Deva

Elite Roman legions invaded Britain in AD43 and were sent across the country to subdue the tribes and establish strongholds. One legion headed northwest and found a perfect site, a sandstone ridge overlooking and controlling a navigable river. It was within easy striking distance of the wild Ordovice tribe in the North Wales Mountains and the Brigande tribes in the Pennines.

They dug in and founded Deva; when they started is not certain but their fortress was completed by Agricola in AD78–79. It became the main home of the 20th Valeria Victrix Legion for over 200 years and, 1600 years later, we can still see their superlatives.

The best of these is the Amphitheatre. Just southeast of the present city centre, it is the largest Roman amphitheatre found in Britain and the northern half has been fully uncovered. Other Ro-

The Rows

The centre of the city was largely destroyed by fire in 1278, and this destruction might have been a factor in the creation of a superlative unique to Chester – the Rows. They are a series of covered walkways with stalls, built above existing ground-floor shops, which are not really at ground level but are sunk a few steps below.

Whatever the explanation, they can only be found in Chester, were built between 1327 and the early 1700s and their black-and-white frontages give Bridge Street, Eastgate Street and Watergate Street a distinctive appearance.

The Roodee

Chester also has a superlative in its racecourse. The Roodee was built on the infilled Roman port and was used as a place for grazing animals, training troops and playing sports. In the early 16th century, the City Assembly decided that the sports being played, particularly football, were too dangerous and should be replaced. Horse racing was one of the alternatives and started in 1540, the first recorded horse racing in the UK.

Blackpool

Blackpool was once a tiny fishing village and has now become an institution. Its prosperity was brought about by the industrialization of the North West, the arrival of railways and the foresight of its citizens. A few statistics tell the story:

● The first recorded visitors came to the village in 1735 – they stayed at a cottage owned by Ethart A. Whiteside.
● The first amusement arcade, Uncle Tom's Cabin, opened in 1750. ● The railway was completed on 29th April, 1846. ● The first pier (North Pier) opened in 1863. ● The electric Tramway opened on 29th September, 1885. ● Blackpool Tower opened in 1894.

Above: Blackpool, Lancashire.

Today, Blackpool attracts 16 800 000 visitors per year generating £435 000 000 – more than all the Greek Islands and mainland Greece combined; there are 3 500 hotels, guest houses and holiday flats, containing 120 000 holiday beds – more than in the whole of Portugal.

Over the years, Blackpool has boasted the world's first electric arc streetlighting, the world's first electric street-tramway, Britain's tallest building and Britain's largest theatre.

Blackpool Tower

Blackpool Tower, a 158 m (519 ft) replica of the Eiffel Tower, opened in 1894 and as it approaches its centenary it still attracts more than 1 400 000 paying visitors every year, making it one of the top ten admission-charging attractions in Britain.

The continued popularity of the town is demonstrated by two of today's superlatives. Blackpool Pleasure Beach is Britain's most-visited free attraction, with over 6 500 000 visitors in 1990.

Blackpool Illuminations is the largest free show in Britain; every autumn the town spends over £1 500 000 creating a show involving more than 500 000 different lamps strung on more than 1 000 poles, using more than 120 km (75 miles) of cables.

Manchester

Manchester is one of the North West's vibrant industrial towns with several superlatives of its own . . .

Canals

There are many claimants for the title of the first canal in England, including the Roman Fossdyke at Lincoln, the Exeter Navigation Canal and the Sankey Brook Navigation, but the first true canal under the definition 'an artificial watercourse for inland navigation' was the Duke of Bridgewater's Canal from his coalmines at Worsley to Manchester. It

The Bridgewater Canal, Worsley.

was built for the Duke by James Brindley and opened in 1761, including a complex network of underground colliery canals linked into the main canal, and Brindley constructed an aqueduct to take the Canal over the River Irwell. The completion of the Canal resulted in

Coronation Street

To many in this country and around the world, Manchester and the North West means Coronation Street, the TV soap that is the longest-running domestic drama serial. Starting life on 9 December 1960, 'The Street' recorded its 2000th episode in August, 1990.

Producers Granada TV have capitalized on this by creating Granada Studio Tours, Europe's first and largest television theme park. Opened in July, 1988, it has already attracted over 2 million visitors – hardly surprising considering that you can see how a studio works, sit in Sherlock Holmes' house and have a pint in the Rovers Return.

a dramatic fall in the price of coal in central Manchester.

By the sea

By the end of the Victorian era, Manchester was at the height of its eminence. The Manchester City Fathers decided to capitalize on this with the development of a ship canal, which would convert the city into a port and allow ocean-going vessels to sail into the heart of the city.

A ship canal is very different from a normal canal for barges and narrow boats: in order to allow ships of up to 15 000 tons to use it, the ship canal would need a minimum depth of 8.5 m (28 ft). It was built between 1887 and 1894 and is 64 km (39.7 miles) long – the longest ship canal in Britain and still the eighth longest in the world.

Amongst its many engineering problems was one created by James Brindley

and the Duke of Bridgewater's Canal. Brindley's aqueduct over the River Irwell had to be replaced, but the designers achieved a unique solution by building the Barton Swing Aqueduct to replace Brindley's structure. It is a lock system on the Bridgewater Canal that, on closing, becomes a cast-iron box 72 m (235 ft) long, 5.5 m (18 ft) wide and 1.8 m (6 ft) deep, encloses a section of canal and swings to allow passage on the ship canal below it. It was opened on 21st August, 1893.

On the Rails

The Victorian era was the 'age of the train' and the two great cities of the North West were involved in railway development from the early days. George Stephenson built his *Rocket* in 1825 to compete in (and win) the Rainhill Trials in 1826, and in 1830 he opened the world's first commercial passenger service, the Liverpool to

Manchester Railway. The Manchester terminal of the line was the Liverpool Road Station, the world's first passenger railway station. For some years it languished as a goods station and yard but it has now been restored as the Manchester Museum of Science and Industry. The Museum also contains the world's largest display of working stationary steam engines.

The Imperial Arch

Manchester has always welcomed industrious newcomers from all over the world and one such example can be found in the city's Chinatown. The dynamic bustle of this area of the city centre is reflected in the Imperial Arch, 9.2 m (30 ft) tall and decorated with gold leaf and ceramic dragons. It is the largest Chinese gateway in Europe and was built by a team flown in from Peking.

Liverpool

Liverpool can trace its origins back to AD100 and was chartered in the early part of the 13th century, but its growth into a great seaport and cosmopolitan city really started in the 18th century and its greatest superlatives all date from the 20th century.

The Royal Liver Building

The Royal Liver Building's place in history is not guaranteed by the *Liver Birds*, although they are nearly 6 m (19 ft) tall and stand 98.5 m (322 ft) above sea level; it is guaranteed by the Royal Liver Clock. The clock was installed in the left-hand tower of the Royal Liver Building in July, 1911, and has four dials. Each dial has a diameter of 7.7 m (25 ft) which is 76 cm (2½ ft) wider than Big Ben. Each minute hand is 4.3 m (14 ft) long and up to 1 m (3 ft) wide, and the dials are 67.5 m (220 ft) above ground level.

Albert Docks

Nearby are the Albert Docks, built by Jesse Hartley between 1841 and 1848,

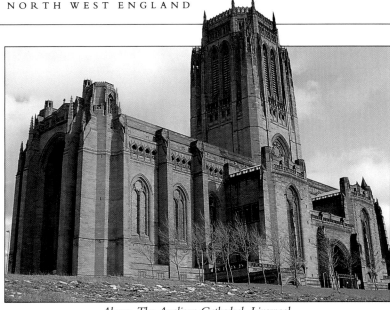
Above: The Anglican Cathedral, Liverpool.

but it is their restoration over the last decade that has turned them into a superlative. The docks represent the largest group of Grade 1 listed buildings in Britain with 3 hectares (7½ acres) of docks enclosed by a series of five-storey warehouses containing 120 000 km² (1.3 million sq. ft) of floor space. The warehouses now contain museums and art galleries, including the northern outpost of the Tate Gallery, and many leisure and eating places. The docks claim approximately 5 millions visitors a year which would make them the second-most-popular free attraction in the country.

Cathedrals

Liverpool's crowning glories are its cathedrals – both of which were built during the 20th century. The Roman Catholic Metropolitan Cathedral is famous for its 'wigwam' design and has the largest display of stained glass in Britain, weighing over 2000 tons.

The C of E Liverpool Cathedral is the largest cathedral in Britain; it is 190 m (619 ft) long, 54 m (175 ft) at its widest and 102 m (331 ft) tall and has the largest gothic tower arches in the world. Its designer was Giles Gilbert Scott, who won a competition for its design when

he was 21 years old. (He also designed the classic British red telephone box.) Building started when Edward VII laid the foundation stone in 1904 but it was not completed until 1978.

The Cathedral also possesses the largest organ in Europe containing 9704 pipes ranging from 2.5 cm (1 in) to 10 m (32 ft). The lowest 'C' pipe weighs more than a ton. The organ was built in Liverpool by Henry Willis and Sons. The cathedral also has the heaviest and highest peal of bells in the world with 13 bells weighing 16H tons.

The Mersey Tunnel

The Mersey Tunnel is another Liverpool superlative that deserves a mention, if only for the number of zeros involved in many of its statistics. The Queensway Tunnel is the longest road tunnel in Britain and was opened by George V in 1934. It is 4.6 km (2.87 miles) long with an internal diameter of 13.3 m (44 ft). Its construction involved the use of 254 550 kg (560 000 lb) of explosives to remove 1 200 000 tons of rock and clay; during the construction 34 000 000 000 litres (7 500 00 000 gallons) of water had to be pumped from the workings and the cast iron linings are held in place by 1 000 000 bolts.

East Midlands

Parks and Palaces, Fountains and Forts . . . and Butlins

The East Midlands are often described as 'the Shires of Middle England'. They stretch from the North Sea coast to the Peak District and include Lincolnshire, Nottinghamshire, Derbyshire, Leicestershire and Northamptonshire.

The landscape ranges from the fenlands around Spalding through the remnants of Sherwood Forest to the dales of Derbyshire and the heights of Kinder Scout.

Man's influence in the area can be seen by megalithic remains in the Peak District, Roman and medieval relics in Lincoln, great houses built from Tudor times onwards and the seaside resorts of the 19th and 20th centuries. The last 50 years have also seen the creation of the Peak District National Park and the flooding of Rutland Water.

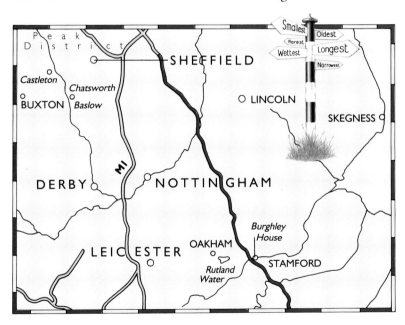

The Peak District

National Park

The Peak District National Park was the first national park to be created in Britain. Indeed, the mass trespasses of Kinder Scout were one of the major factors in the opening up of the countryside to the general public.

The Park was officially designated on 17 April, 1951, and covers an area 1404 km² (542 sq. miles). Due to its position in the middle of the country, surrounded by the cities of Manchester, Bradford,

Opposite: Kinder Scout.

Leeds, Huddersfield, Sheffield, Nottingham, Derby and Stoke-on-Trent, it is estimated that nearly 20 million people live within 50 miles of the Park. As a result of this, the Peak District is the most visited of the National Parks with around 20 000 000 visitors every year. There is certainly a great deal for them to see.

Caves and Gems

Castleton lies on the A625 midway between Manchester and Sheffield. It is an obvious centre for walkers, being just south of the start of the Pennine Way at Edale, southeast of Kinder Scout (the Peak District's highest point at 636 m (2088 ft)), in the shadow of Mam Tor (the Shivering Mountain) and Winnants Pass, but it is the combination of caves, mines and a unique mineral, that makes Castleton famous.

The Peak Cavern has the largest natural cave opening in Britain – the entrance is 10 m (33 ft) high and 30 m (100 ft) wide and leads to an extensive cave system. In fact, the entrance is so large that, until the 1850s, it contained a row of cottages.

Above: Blue John Cavern.

The Speedwell Cavern is a disused lead mine, which was developed in the 1770s by John Gilbert, with underground canals leading to the mine faces. The

Good Morning Campers!

Skegness, on the Lincolnshire coast, is a typical seaside resort. It was developed from 1780 onwards and is normally associated with John Hassall's brilliant 1910 railway poster showing a jolly man with a hat, pipe, scarf and wellingtons dancing on a beach with the punch line, 'Skegness is so bracing'.

However, Skegness does have one further call to fame. A new concept in mass-market holidays for workers was pioneered there, in 1937, when Billy Butlin opened his first Butlin's Holiday Camp. Holiday-makers were invited to book into residential chalets for a week, with all meals and entertainments included in the price and everything organised and 'jollied along' by professional helpers, from the moment they woke them up until they sang the last song.

Above: Royal Devonshire Hospital.

mine was unsuccessful but visitors to Speedwell now have the unique experience of touring the underground cavern by boat.

Castleton's two other mines are the Blue John Cavern and the Treak Cliff Cavern. Both are now show caves although some limited mining still takes place. Mining for Blue John has gone on in the caverns for the last two to three hundred years, (Blue John is a unique substance which was created when the mineral fluorspar was infiltrated by hydrocarbons). The hydrocarbons, mainly oil, penetrated the crystal planes of the mineral giving it a bluish-purple hue of varying intensity dependent upon the concentration of hydrocarbons. Over the centuries it has been much prized for jewellery and also for larger items. Nearby Chatsworth House has the largest vase ever made from a single piece of Blue John.

Palace of the Peak

Chatsworth House is the home of the Duke of Devonshire. Construction of this magnificent house was started in 1549 by Sir William Cavendish. It was re-built by the first Duke in 1687 and radically re-structured for the fourth Duke by James Paine, between 1756 and 1763. The fourth Duke also hired 'Capability' Brown, in 1761, to re-design the 445 ha (1100 acre) Park. The sixth Duke made some alterations to the

Opposite: The Emperor Fountain at Chatsworth House.

house in 1822, but his main contribution was to the gardens, particularly to the waterworks there.

He hired Joseph Paxton (who was later to design The Crystal Palace) as head gardener. Unfortunately, two of Paxton's great creations have subsequently been demolished – the Great Conservatory and the Lily House. However, his greatest creation at Chatsworth is still working. The Emperor Fountain was built in 1843 and is fed by water collected in a 3 ha (8 acre) lake on the hillside behind the house. The fountain was first run on 1 June, 1844, and reached a height of 79 m (260 ft), the tallest fountain in Britain. It is still run today, although infrequently and rarely above 60 m (200 ft) high.

Buxton

Buxton is a delightful town 305 m (1000 ft) above sea level, which has been attracting visitors for nearly 2000 years and has benefited enormously from the patronage of the Dukes of Devonshire.

Buxton spa waters emerge from their underground source at a constant 28°C (82°F) and their 'medicinal' properties have been recognised since Roman times.

The town has a fine imitation of Bath's Royal Crescent, which was built around the natural spring in 1780 and called The Crescent. Behind The Crescent

are the Opera House, restored and now in use, and the Royal Devonshire Hospital.

The Hospital was originally built as stables for the hotel in The Crescent and was converted in 1858. The stables open courtyard was covered in 1881 with a spectacular, single unsupported dome which has a diameter of 50 m (164 ft) and is the largest in England.

East of Buxton, on Taddington Moor, lies clear evidence of early man's involvement with the area. Five Wells is a 4000-year-old megalithic tomb. At a height of 427 m (1400 ft), it is the highest stone-age tomb in England.

Rutland

One of the casualties of the 1974 reorganisation of English local government was the eradication of the country's smallest county. Rutland was subsumed into Leicestershire but – nearly 20 years on – Rutland still refuses to die.

Rutland Water

A great deal of what was Rutland has disappeared under water. The river Gwash was dammed in 1970 to provide water for the Anglian Water area and the resulting lake was called Rutland Water.

Rutland often claims to be the largest artificial lake in Britain, but that honour goes to Kielder Water in Northumbria which has a greater capacity and circumference. However, because the landscape of Rutland is much flatter than the North Tyne valley, the actual surface area of Rutland Water – at 1254 ha (3100 acres) – is significantly greater than Kielder, 168 ha (416 acres) larger to be precise, making it the artificial lake covering the largest area in Europe and the second largest surface area lake in England, second to Windermere.

Oakham Castle

Rutland's former county town, Oakham, lies just to the west of Rutland Water. It contains many reminders of the old county, including the Great Hall of Oakham Castle. The Castle was built in the 12th century and the Hall was used for banqueting and was unusual in that it was free-standing from the castle walls.

The rest of the castle has now disappeared but the Hall is the best-preserved Norman hall in Britain. It contains a unique collection of horseshoes because of a local byelaw stating that any peer of the realm travelling through Oakham must present a ceremonial horseshoe for display there. The collection now runs into hundreds, with horseshoes from peers, princes and monarchs.

Burghley House

East of Rutland Water is the Georgian town of Stamford, and just south of the town is Burghley House. It was built by Elizabeth I's advisor, William Cecil, and was constructed between 1553 and 1587. It is the largest Tudor house in Britain, and one room in the House, the Heaven Room (painted by Verrio), is considered the finest painted room in Britain.

Lincoln

As a city, Lincoln has been a significant centre since the Romans realised the strategic importance of the site in the early days after the Roman invasion.

Lincoln Cathedral

Lincoln Cathedral's mighty west front, with its twin towers, built on Lincoln Edge, dominates the city and survived an earthquake in 1185 that destroyed the rest of the Norman Cathedral.

It was re-built from 1192 onwards and is one of the largest and most beautiful cathedrals in Britain. Its Chapter House, built in 1420, is a ten-sided polygon, the first polygonal chapter house ever built in Britain.

Below: Rutland Water, surface area 416 acres.

The library next to it was built at the same time and contains a priceless collection of books and manuscripts, including one of the four original Magna Carta parchments.

Lindum Colonia

The original Roman legion fort is buried under the foundations of Lincoln Castle but excavations have shown that it was one of the first to be founded after the invasion, probably around AD50. By 300, the original fortress had developed into *Lindum Colonia*, a major town that was probably founded by retired legionnaires and their families. The town was heavily fortified and the north gate of the town, Newport Arch, is unique in that it is the only Roman gateway in Britain that is still standing, with its arch in place and capable of being driven through.

The Fossdyke

Lincoln's largest Roman remain was created around AD100. The Fossdyke is an 17.7 km (11 mile) long navigable ditch dug to link the River Witham to the River Trent. It is the earliest canal in Britain, pre-dating the Exeter Navigation Canal by nearly 1500 years. At the Lincoln end, the waterway broadens out to form Brayford Pool.

Lincoln Castle

Lincoln Castle dates from 1068 and was one of the first Norman castles built after the Conquest.

Today, the castle walls enclose a wooded lawn and two sets of buildings. The first, built by John Carr in 1787, housed the County Gaol until 1878, and includes a unique prisoners' chapel where all of the pew seats have high sides and backs and self-locking single doors so that when the prisoner was in his pew, he was surrounded by high wooden walls and could only see the pulpit and altar. The second dates from 1823 and was built by Sir Robert Smirke. It used to house the Assize Courts and is now the home of Lincoln County Court.

Opposite: The Heaven Room at Burghley House.

Yorkshire and Humberside

Ancient Cities, a Mighty Bridge and Fish and Chips

The Yorkshire and Humberside region contains beautiful and dramatic countryside in the Dales, Moors and Wolds, and a coastline that varies from the imposing heights of Boulby Cliffs and Flamborough Head to fast-eroding Holderness and ever-changing Spurn Head.

The City of York has been shaped, built and re-built successively by Roman, Saxon, Viking, Norman, Medieval and more recent hands and has preserved fine examples from each period. However, York is by no means the only location for superlative architecture in the region. In other parts of the area, you can find castles and abbeys, and Britain's oldest city.

There is also a bridge so large that the curvature of the earth had to be taken into account when it was being built; probably the largest golf balls in the world, and a cinema screen that is bigger than the floor-space of most modern cinemas.

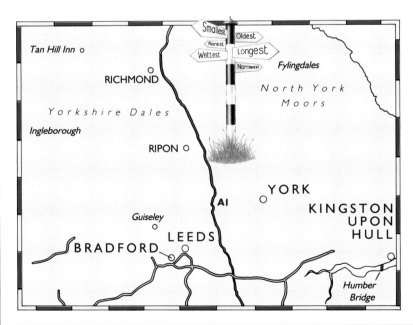

The Yorkshire Dales

The Yorkshire Dales, part of the Pennines, were created a National Park in 1954. (The Park covers 1762 km^2 – 680 sq. miles – of beautiful and photogenic countryside.)

Above: The Tan Hill Inn.

The Dales are a series of hills and heights cut by fast-flowing streams; over thousands of years the flowing water has eroded and dissolved the limestone slopes of the heights to create a classic karst landscape of limestone pavements, swallow holes, caves and collapsed caverns.

Ingleborough Hill

Ingleborough Hill is a brooding, flat-topped height overlooking the villages of Ingleton and Clapham. It is only 724 m (2373 ft) high but on its summit stand the remains of the highest Iron-Age fort in Britain. The ramparts and fortifications were used by local tribes around AD70 as they tried to resist the Roman invaders.

Gaping Gill

The slopes of Ingleborough are made of carboniferous limestone and are riddled with openings leading to one of the Dales' many extensive cave systems, the Gaping Gill/Ingleborough System.

This network is unique because of Gaping Gill, a hole in the ground into which Fell Beck disappears following its flow down Ingleborough towards Clapham. The water drops vertically for 111 m (365 ft) into a chamber that is approximately 150 m (500 ft) by 30 m (100 ft). Gaping Gill is the longest waterfall in England and the second longest in Britain.

The Ease Gill System

North of Ingleborough is Whernside, another height, less spectacular than Ingleborough but higher at 736 m (2419 ft). The slopes of Whernside hide another spectacular set of caves, the Ease Gill System. It is still being explored but Ease Gill already extends through 66 km (41 miles) of caverns and passages and is the longest cave system in Britain.

Take the High Road

About 40 km (25 miles) northeast of Ingleborough a lonely minor road heads north from the village of Keld into the hills and round into Arkengarthdale. The road often gets blocked by snow for weeks at a time but it is worth travelling along because you are sure of a warm welcome. On the road, at a height of 528 m (1723 ft), you will find the Tan Hill Inn, Britain's highest public house.

Richmond Castle

The River Swale flows out of the Dales and through the town of Richmond. The town is dominated by its Castle. Time has taken its toll on the Castle but it has the distinction of never having been attacked by an opposing army.

Below: Richmond Castle.

Fountains Abbey, North Yorkshire.

Fish and Chips

Guiseley is a town on the road from Leeds to Ilkley. It is also the home of Harry Ramsden's.

Harry founded his fish and chip shop in 1928 and his reputation as a purveyor of delicious fish and chips soon spread. To meet demand, Harry needed more staff and more room.

Harry Ramsden's Fish & Chip Shop at White Cross in Guiseley is now the largest fish and chip restaurant in the world. It employs 140 staff, who serve 1 000 000 customers every year, and they eat their way through an incredible 213 tons of fish and 356 tons of potatoes per year.

place, shops and stalls once occupied part of the church building. Since 1971, the church has been divided into two, with one half still serving as the parish church and the other forming the regimental museum for the Green Howards Regiment.

Ripon

Many people are surprised to learn that the oldest city in Britain is not York, but Ripon.

Ripon only has a population of around 12 000 but it is nevertheless a city and proud of it. Its charter was awarded by Alfred the Great in 886 and was the first city charter granted in Britain. By comparison, London was chartered in 1066 and York in 1396.

Ripon's Cathedral of St. Peter and St. Wilfrid was founded by Wilfrid in 655 and became a bishopric in 672. Norman and subsequent re-building means that nothing of Wilfrid's original Saxon church remains above ground, but the crypt is a spectacular Saxon relic and dates from 681.

Setting the Watch
One particular Ripon tradition which has continued for more than 1000 years involves the Ripon Wakeman. In a

Below: The Ripon Wakeman.

The Castle was founded by Alan the Red in 1080; its curtain walls are 3 m (10 ft) thick and are the oldest original castle walls in Britain still standing.

The Castle's great hall is called Scolland's Hall; it was erected in 1090 and is the oldest stone hall in Britain. The great tower was built on top of an existing gateway in 1150 and is 30 m (100 ft) tall with walls up to 3.5m (12 ft) thick.
Holy Trinity Church
Richmond's Holy Trinity Church is unique. Situated in Richmond market

Above: The Fylingdales.

ceremony known as Setting the Watch, he blows a horn in the market square at 9 pm every evening to indicate to the townspeople that he is taking care of their city for the night.

Fountains Abbey

Six-and-a-half kilometres (4 miles) southwest of Ripon is one of Britain's greatest religious remains. The ruins of Fountains Abbey are so magnificent that you cannot help but wonder what it might have been like today, if it wasn't for Henry VIII and the subsequent ravages of time.

The Abbey was founded as the home of a group of monks in 1134 and named a house of the Cistercian order in 1150. Its fortune was made from trading in wool, and over the centuries it became the richest religious establishment in Britain.

Successive abbots used the Abbey's income to build and extend it, and construction went on almost continuously between 1150 and 1526. By the end of that period, it had become the largest set of religious buildings in Britain. In 1539, at the height of its power, Henry VIII dissolved the monasteries and Fountains Abbey was emptied and sold. Subsequent owners used its beautiful buildings as a cheap source of building stones.

Bridging the Humber

The early 1960s saw the completion of some of the greatest bridge engineering projects ever undertaken in Britain. The Forth Road Bridge was opened in 1964 and the Severn Road Bridge in 1966. In fact, there was only one major British estuary that remained unbridged – the Humber. Crossing it would be a colossal undertaking. Considering that the Forth Bridge was just over 1000 m long between its two suspension towers, the Humber Bridge would need to be nearly half as long again – the longest bridge in the world.

Below: The world's longest bridge – the Humber.

The decision to build it was announced on 22 January, 1966, although work did not commence until 27 July, 1972. It took almost eight years to bridge the estuary and a further year to complete the finishing work, but the Humber Bridge was finally opened by Elizabeth II on 17 July, 1981.

Vital Statistics

The bridge's statistics tell their own story. It is the longest suspension bridge in the world and the longest bridge span in the world at 112 m (367 ft) longer than its nearest rival. The length between the two suspension towers is 1410 m (4626 ft). When the side road spans to the north and south of the bridge are included, the total length of the bridge structure is 2220 m (7283 ft or 1.38 miles) and the tops of the two suspension towers are each 162.5 m (5333 ft 1⅜ in) above mean sea level. Due to the scale of the structure, the two towers had to be offset 36 mm (1⅜ in) from parallel to allow for the curvature of the earth.

Fore!

The North Yorkshire Moors National Park was founded in 1952 and covers 1433 km² (553 sq. miles) of rugged, treeless moorland and coast. It is a tranquil, peaceful park with barrows, crosses and ruins providing evidence of Man's presence on the moors over the centuries. But, if you drive across the moors on the B1416 south of Whitby, you could get quite a surprise . . .

When three huge golf balls appear before you on the moors, don't pinch yourself – you are not dreaming. The Fylingdales, as they called, are each 47 m (154 ft) in diameter and weigh 100 tons. The Missile Early Warning Station was constructed in 1961 at the

The National Museum of Photography, Film and Television, Bradford.

height of the Cold War. It is one of three built around the world – the others are in Greenland and Alaska, to give warning of sneak attacks. An anachronism in the new world of the 1990s but somehow over thirty years they seem to have settled into the moorland landscape. They are unique in Britain and certainly a superlative.

Square Eyes

Bradford is the home of one of the most interesting new museums in Britain, the National Museum of Photography, Film and Television.

Naturally, given the subjects it covers, the Museum has a cinema screen. This, however, is not any old screen – it is the IMAX cinema screen. At 19 m (62 ft) wide, it is the biggest in Britain.

York

Eboracum – Eferwic – Jorvik – York

The Swale, Ure and Nidd flow eastwards out of the Yorkshire Dales, turn south and each in turn join the Yorkshire Ouse which flows down to the Humber and out to the North Sea. The broad valley they form between the Dales and the Moors provides an excellent corridor to the North. The point where the Fosse joins the Ouse is the lowest position where the river is easily fordable or bridgeable and also the highest point of navigation for reasonably sized boats. The importance of this communications nodal point and the need to control it has been recognised since pre-historic times and, almost 2000 years ago, the Romans built a fortress there which evolved into a city that is rich in history.

However, although York's greatest treasures span from Roman to medieval times, it is by no means a 'preserved' city; it has continued to develop and change to the present day.

During the 18th century, it was a major stop on the coaching routes to the North, and the great chocolate and confectionary businesses, with which the city is still associated, were founded in the 1760s.

Eboracum

The Romans called York *Eboracum*. Initially, they built one of their major fortresses as a home base for one of the three élite Roman legions stationed in Britain, but a major town soon developed around the fortress. *Eboracum's* importance was shown by a visit from Emperor Constantius in AD306 and the fact that his son, Constantine the Great, was first proclaimed Emperor in *Eboracum*.

Re-development

York has developed and been re-built many times on the same site and consequently much of Roman York has been destroyed or re-used. For example, York Minster is built on top of the foundations of the original fortress. Excavation in the city has revealed a wealth of remains, particularly under the Minster, but there are signs of the Roman origins in many parts of the city. The largest above-ground remain is the Multangular Tower which was built in the 4th century and formed part of the perimeter defences of the fortress.

Eferwic

In Anglo-Saxon times York was known as *Eferwic*. The first Church of St. Peter in York was built in 627 and the first Bishop of York was created in 664. Also during the 7th century, St. Peter's School was founded, the third oldest school in Britain. The archbishopric was created in 735.

Jorvik

York's Saxon links were abruptly terminated in 867 when the city was captured by Viking invaders and became part of Danelaw. It was re-named *Jorvik* and continued to be a very important centre, but the Vikings were not great builders and no substantial remains of the period were discovered until 1973, when reconstruction work was undertaken in the vaults of a bank building in Coppergate.

Left: Jorvik Viking Centre.

Viking Centre

The excavators uncovered a number of Viking timber buildings that had been buried in wet peat, preserved so well that furniture and implements from the period could be re-assembled. This discovery is celebrated at the Jorvik Viking Centre in Coppergate, an exhibition that accurately reconstructs the day-to-day life in a typical *Jorvik* street 1000 years ago. Understandably, it is now one of York's major tourist attractions.

York

With the ending of Danelaw in 954, York was once again absorbed into Saxon England. Then, in 1066, William the Conqueror arrived.

Following the Conquest, William suppressed opposition in the north of England and built two castles to control York.

York Minster

In 1069, the existing Minster was badly damaged by fire and a new, massive Norman Minster was built in its place. Work on this new building started in 1070. However, the Minster lasted only a few years before successive archbishops started extending and re-building it. In particular, Archbishop Walter de Grey decided that a religious centre second only to Canterbury needed something more imposing and reconstruction work started in 1220 and continued until 1472.

Over the course of more than 250 years, builders created the largest Gothic cathedral in the whole of northern Europe. The completed Minster is 160 m (524 ft) long and at its widest (across the transepts) it measures 76 m (249 ft). The last major building project was the completion of the Central Tower which is 71 m (234 ft) high.

Majestic though the Minster is, its greatest glory is undoubtedly its stained glass. The Catholic Cathedral at Liverpool contains more glass but York Minster has an incomparable collection of 800 years of glass, including windows from every period from the 12th century to the present day. The glass includes the oldest piece in Britain, a section of a Jesse window made around 1150, and the Great East Window; created at the start of the 15th century, it is the largest single area of medieval glass in the world.

York Minster has been continuously maintained and restored, particularly following serious fires in 1829 and 1840. A major restoration programme to strengthen its foundations was undertaken between 1967 and 1972 and the most recent work followed another

Below: York Minster.

major fire in 1984. But miraculously, the Minster has survived the War of the Roses, Henry VIII, the Civil War and, most recently, the Second World War. It is York's top tourist attraction and, in 1990, it was visited by 2 500 000 people, as many people as visited St. Paul's Cathedral in London, making it the eighth most popular free tourist attraction in Britain.

The City Walls

At about the same time as work on the new Minster commenced (1220), work also started on building York's City Walls.

The Walls had a circumference of about 5 km (3 miles) with fortified gates called 'Bars' allowing access to the City at regular intervals. Walmgate Bar is the only city or town gate in Britain whose barbican has been preserved complete, showing how strong York's defences were.

Today, there are gaps in the Walls but what remains allows a perfect platform for viewing York, particularly the section from St. Cuthbert's round to Bootham Bar, with views of the Minster and Deanery Gardens.

The Shambles

South of the Minster, in the heart of the old walled city, medieval York is seen at its best. Two streets in particular, Stonegate and The Shambles, give a clear indication of what the street-scene must have been like in the 14th and 15th centuries.

The Shambles is mentioned in the Domesday Book and is regarded as the best-preserved medieval street in Europe.

The Merchant Adventurer's Hall

Close to The Shambles is the Merchant Adventurers' Hall, a guild hall.

The Guild was founded in 1357 and the oldest part of the Hall, Trinity Chapel, dates from 1368, although most of the building is 15th-century. It is a clear indication of the power and wealth of the merchants in medieval York and is the oldest surviving guild hall in Britain.

Right: The stained glass, York Minster.

The Railways

In Victorian times, the importance of the Vale of York corridor to the North was recognised by the railway engineers. The York city fathers, particularly George Hudson, were astute enough to ensure that York became one of the major stations on the East Coast line from London to Edinburgh and an important railway centre. The first London to York train ran in 1840, and the great Victorian railway station, built by Thomas Prosser, was opened in 1877.

The link between York and the railways is reinforced today by the National Railway Museum. It adjoins York's Victorian railway station and presents the story of railways from the 1820s to the present day, including many of the great British locomotives, and displays ranging from the royal coaches to railway ephemera. It is the largest railway museum in Europe.

*The Merchant Adventurers'
Hall – mostly 15th-century.*

Northumbria

Walls and Water, Christianity, Castles and Railways

Northumbria is the beautiful, rugged border region between England and Scotland. This beauty is reflected in the Northumberland National Park, the Cheviot Hills, Kielder Forest and Water, and some breathtaking waterfalls.

Because of its location, picturesque Northumbria has been fought over for thousands of years and the area is littered with military relics, including the greatest Roman remains in Britain and some of the best-preserved castles and fortifications in the country.

It was also the cradle of Christianity in England, thanks to St. Aidan, St. Cuthbert and St. Wilfrid, a heritage that led to the creation of the Prince Bishops of Durham and the rich architecture they constructed over the centuries.

Northumbria has been a land of great builders since Hadrian in AD122, a tradition that has been continued over the last 300 years by bridge builders, railway engineers and, in the last decade, the builders of the biggest shopping centre in Europe.

Kielder Water

While neighbouring Cumbria is famous for its Lake District, Northumbria has no large natural lakes but has made up for this by creating the largest man-made lake in Europe – Kielder Water.

Kielder was created by damming and flooding the North Tyne Valley. The dam is 1.2 km (3/4 mile) long and 52 m (170 ft) high and was completed in late 1980.

On 15 December, 1980, the flow from the River North Tyne was turned off, reputedly for the first time since the last Ice Age, and re-directed through a sluice in the dam. Kielder Water took 18 months to fill, hardly surprising given that it contains 2000 million hl (44 000 million gallons) of water, has a perimeter of 43.4 km (27 miles) and a surface area of 10.85 km² (4.19 sq. miles).

To complete the Kielder picture, the supply tunnel from the Water's pumping station to Eggleston on the Tees is 30.6 km (19 miles) long – the longest in Britain.

Kielder Water is in the middle of Kielder Forest, the largest forest in Britain and the largest artificially-planted forest in Europe, covering an area of 393.68 km² (152 sq. miles).

Left: Hadrian's Wall.

Waterfalls

Every waterfall enthusiast should visit the River Tees between Middleton in Teesdale and Cow Green Reservoir. Over a stretch of river running less than 16 km (10 miles) there are three remarkable waterfalls caused by the Tees crossing outcrops of the Great Whin Sill.

Cascades

Low Force is a series of cascades immediately above Wynch Bridge. Further north is High Force, the biggest waterfall in England in terms of water flow. Running off the moors, the Tees creates a rugged gorge before it plunges 21 m (70 ft) over Whin Sill in a single drop into a pool almost as deep again.

Further upstream, the Tees crosses Whin Sill for the first time, at Cauldron Snout, a spectacular series of cascades dropping the river 60 m (200 ft).

Roman Remains

Roman remains across Northumbria include forts, baths, villas and roads and, as most were built between 1900 and 1700 years ago, they show that the Romans were truly master builders.

In the early decades of the conquest, Agricola (AD40–93) wanted to subjugate the entire island to Rome, but wiser counsel arrived in Britain during the second century.

Hadrian's Wall

Emperor Hadrian arrived in AD122 to survey his distant outpost and decided that 'enough was enough'. To fight and

Below: High Force Falls.

subdue the Picts and Scots in their own highland glens would have required more manpower than the empire could afford. It was better to contain them, and he ordered the construction of a mighty wall to mark the edge of the empire.

Hadrian's Wall was an engineering enterprise to compare with any 20th-century project. The completed wall cut across the narrow neck of England from Newcastle to Carlisle. It was to be 80 Roman miles (122 km/76 miles) long, an average of 4.5 m (15 ft) high and 3 m (10 ft) wide with milecastles (small forts) roughly every Roman mile, large garrison forts every 10 Roman miles, a ditch to the north of the wall, a military road just south of the wall and supply bases and naval bases in the rear. It involved around 30 000 construction workers, including the three élite Roman legions in Britain, and took about 20 years to build. There is also evidence of considerable strengthening and rebuilding of the Wall around AD200.

The remains visible today form the greatest Roman relic in the whole of northern Europe. The line of the Wall is clear – it often follows the Great Whin Sill, and there are frequent, well-preserved sections. Excavations have revealed details of the milecastles, forts and the civilian communities that developed to supply the Wall garrisons.

Vercovicium (or Housesteads, as it is called today) is just off the B6318 east of Haltwhistle and was probably a major fort on the Wall. The preserved remains are enclosed by walls and inside these are the foundations of the headquarters building, soldiers' quarters, latrines and granaries. The granaries include evidence of the Romans' sophisticated storing and drying systems with under-floor airflows. *Vercovicium* and the sections of Hadrian's Wall on either side of it were built on one of the Whin Sill outcrops and provide spectacular views.

Bamburgh Castle

Bamburgh Castle is a spectacular structure on the Northumbrian coast, over-

Twenty-first-century Shopping and Leisure

At the end of the 1970s, Sir John Hall had a vision – he wanted to blend the best of American shopping-mall technology with the British tradition of shopping on a smaller scale with friendly, helpful specialist shops and stalls. Furthermore, he wanted to create it in Northumbria.

Work on the 'mall' started in 1984, the first phase opened in April, 1986, and the development was completed in October 1987. The result was the Gateshead MetroCentre – the largest indoor shopping and leisure centre in Europe.

Its 5 km (3 miles) of covered walkways hold 340 shops and 35 stalls, with a total shopping area of 145 000 m² (1 560 000 sq. ft), 50 restaurants and cafes, a bowling alley, cinema and Metroland, Europe's first and largest indoor theme park.

During 1991, the MetroCentre was visited by 26 million people; the busiest day in 1991 was Saturday, 30 November, when just over 200 000 people flocked in.

looking the Farne Islands and Holy Island. It is situated on top of an outcrop of the Great Whin Sill and dominates the area. There is evidence that the site was used in pre-historic times and the Romans undoubtedly recognised the potential of its location.

The first major fortress was built on the site in AD550 by Ida, a local tribal chieftain. Since then, the fortress at Bamburgh has been extended and rebuilt many times and has been used as a royal castle for the coronation of the kings of Northumbria.

The Normans occupied the building and further fortified it, and a Bishop of Durham restored it in the 18th century. In the late 19th century, it was bought by Lord Armstrong, who renovated it again – this time in the Victorian style – to the annoyance of some archeological purists.

The Armstrongs still own and live in Bamburgh and it is a superlative because it has been a changing and developing castle, occupied continuously for nearly 1450 years, a British record.

Berwick-upon-Tweed

There are border towns and there are *border towns* – Berwick-upon-Tweed is definitely a *border town*. The Tweed forms the boundary between England and Scotland and the ownership of Berwick changed hands 14 times between the 12th and 15th centuries. It fell under English rule again in 1482 and has remained there ever since.

Due to its troubled history, Berwick has many military relics, the greatest of which are the Elizabethan ramparts that enclose the old town.

Below: Britain's oldest barracks, Berwick.

Berwick's first town walls were constructed by Edward I in the 1290s but proved insufficient, and Elizabeth I – under the joint threat of French and Scottish invasion from Scotland – constructed between 1558 and 1566 the first town ramparts designed to survive artillery bombardment. The ramparts and gun bastions still encircle the town and are regarded as the finest 16th-century fortifications in Europe.

Under the architect Vanbrugh, the construction of Berwick Barracks, inside the Elizabethan ramparts, began in 1719. They were built when the citizens of Berwick complained about the need to billet the garrison within their own homes and are the oldest barracks in Britain.

Centuries of Christianity

St. Aidan

St. Aidan founded a monastery on Holy Island (Lindisfarne) in AD635. He and his monks arrived from Iona to bring Celtic Christianity to the English.

After Aidan's death, Lindisfarne continued to develop and the Priory became a major religious settlement and cultural centre. The monks there created great works, such as the world-famous Lindisfarne Gospels which are now in the British Museum.

The Priory was destroyed during Henry VIII's dissolution of the monasteries but the ruins and the surroundings are still evocative.

St. Cuthbert

Inspired by a vision of Aidan, St. Cuthbert came to Lindisfarne in AD664. He lived a solitary life on the Farne Islands until his death in 687.

Eleven years later, the monks removed his remains to re-bury them in a specially-prepared spot and discovered that his corpse had not decayed. Thereafter, his relics were considered sacred and were removed from Lindisfarne in 875 to avoid desecration during the frequent Viking raids on the island.

Above: Hexham Abbey.

Monks carried Cuthbert's remains around Northumbria for over 100 years, until they were finally laid to rest in Durham in 997. The present Durham Cathedral dates from 1093 and is regarded as the finest Gothic cathedral in Britain.

St. Wilfred

The third great Northumbrian saint was St. Wilfrid. He lived at around the same time as St. Cuthbert but was a follower of Roman Christianity rather than Celtic. In fact, he triumphed over the Celtic monks at the Synod of Whitby in 663 and became Bishop of Ripon and later Archbishop of York.

He founded a great church at Hexham in 674, which was partially destroyed by Henry VIII. In the foundations of Hexham Abbey, a staircase leads to St. Wilfrid's original crypt from 674. Over 1300 years old, it was constructed from stones pillaged from earlier Roman remains and is the best-preserved Saxon crypt in Britain.

Hexham Abbey also contains St. Wilfrid's Chair which is reputed to be the coronation throne of the Kings of Northumbria and is dated at 681.

The Waggonways

Waggonways were an early transport innovation of the Industrial Revolution, pre-dating canals by 50 years and steam railways by a century.

Coal, iron and other heavy raw materials had to be transported from the mines to the factories. Horse-drawn waggons were the best form of transport available but the heavy loads caused the waggons to sink into the mud. The solution? To floor the waggonways with logs and fix other timbers on top as 'rails' to guide and direct the waggons' wheels. In fact, waggonways, were the forerunners of many 'real' railways with – eventually – the wooden 'rails' being replaced by iron ones, the waggon wheels being replaced by flanged iron wheels and the horses being replaced by steam engines.

To get from the mines to the factories the waggonways had to cross streams and ravines, so bridges capable of carrying heavy loads had to be constructed.

The Causey Arch Bridge

Waggonways were constructed in many parts of the country but the most famous was the Tanfield Waggonway. It ran for 12.9 km (8 miles) from the River Tyne up into the hills to the Tanfield Colliery, and its construction involved the creation of the world's first railway embankment at Causey Burn, and the world's first railway bridge at Causey Arch.

The Causey Arch Bridge, which has been preserved, was built in 1725 by Ralph Wood, a local mason. It has a 32 m (105 ft) span and crosses Beckley Burn at a maximum height of 24.38 m (80 ft) above river level.

The Stockton to Darlington Railway

George Stephenson, the great Victorian engineer, was active in Northumbria. He planned and built the Stockton to Darlington Railway, the first commercial freight railway line in the world.

Below: Holy Island.

Above: Locomotion No. 1.

The line opened on 27 September, 1825, transporting goods between the two towns, but it did not carry paying passengers until 1833, and the honour of being the world's first commercial passenger railway line fell to Stephenson's Liverpool to Manchester line, opened in 1830.

Stephenson also built the locomotives to run on the line and the original engine, called *Locomotion No. 1*, is preserved on the platform at Darlington Railway Station.

Cumbria

Lakes, Mountains and Visitors

Cumbria includes the Lake District, the largest National Park in Britain, and it is here that the highest mountains and largest lakes in England are found. It is an area of great natural beauty and one with many literary associations, including links with Wordsworth, the Lakeland Poets and Beatrix Potter.

This combination of grandeur, beauty and culture makes the area very popular with visitors. Add to this the fact that the M6 clips the eastern edge of the area, giving people in Glasgow, Manchester, Liverpool, Leeds and Birmingham access to the area within a few hours via the motorway network, and you can understand why it is estimated that in 1990 Cumbria received more than 10 000 000 day visitors.

The Park

The Lake District National Park, was founded as one of the first national parks, in 1951. It is the largest, with an area of 2292 km² (885 sq. miles) – only the Snowdonia National Park comes anywhere near to this size. It covers the centre of Cumbria and includes all of the region's most famous lakes and mountains.

Lakes and Tarns

During the last Ice Age a great ice sheet scoured the mountains of Cumbria. It rounded the mountain-tops, over-deepened river valleys and gouged hollows in the sides of the mountains. Tens of thousands of years later, the Lake Dis-

Below: Lake Windermere.

trict emerged – a result of the effects of rainfall and flowing water.

There are hundreds of waters in the Lake District ranging from mighty Windermere to tarns so small or so remote that they have never been named.

It is generally accepted that 16 of the waters are classified as 'the Lakes' and the rest as tarns, although some of the tarns are larger and more popular than some of the lakes.

Windermere

Windermere in the southern Lake District is England's largest lake, although it is only the sixteenth largest in Britain. It covers an area of 14.7 km² (5.69 sq. miles) and is 16.8 km (10.5 miles) long, 1.47 km (1610 yards) wide and 66 m (219 ft) deep at its maximum point.

It is easily the busiest and most popular of the lakes, with boating, water-skiing and swimming and the Lake District's most popular paid-for attraction, the Lake Windermere Steamship.

Opposite Bowness-on-Windermere is Belle Island, a private island on which the first round house ever built in England can be found. Constructed in 1774, it is truly round and is by no means small, containing 20 interconnecting rooms.

Coniston Water

Coniston Water is just to the west of Windermere. It is 8.7 km (5.4 miles)

Above: The Screes.

long and is the fifth largest lake in terms of area.

It is most famous as the scene of world water speed records and, unfortunately, the tragic death of Donald Campbell in *Bluebird* in 1967, as well as being the home of the steam yacht *Gondola*, the oldest working steam yacht in Britain. It was built in 1859 and provided a regular ferry service on the Water until the Second World War. Having been restored by the National Trust, it now takes visitors on regular steam trips.

Wast Water

Wast Water is the deepest lake in England, plunging to a depth of 78 m (258 ft). It is also amongst the most spectacular, surrounded by some of the highest

mountains, with hill sides and scree slopes falling 610 m (1990 ft) almost straight into the lake surface.

. . . More Water!

There are two further notable water superlatives in the region . . .

Scale Force Waterfall at Buttermere has the longest single above-ground drop in England, an unbroken fall of 45 m (148 ft).

Broad Crag Tarn on the side of Scafell Pike has the distinction of being the highest lake in England; the surface of the Tarn is 837m (2748ft) above sea-level.

Mountains

For all except dedicated fell walkers and climbers, the Lake District peaks play a supporting role to the lakes. Nevertheless, they are the most magnificent mountains in England. They are the backdrop for wonderful photographs, looking especially spectacular when snowcapped.

There are only five English peaks over 900 m high and all of them are in Cumbria:

Scafell Pike .... 977 m (3206 ft)

Sca Fell .... 964 m (3162 ft)

Helvellyn .... 953 m (3116 ft)

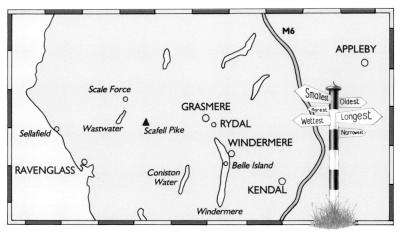

Literature Links

No guide to Cumbrian superlatives can possibly ignore the poets and writers who have been inspired by the beauty of the Lake District. Literary links in the region include Coleridge, De Quincey, Ruskin and Southey but two in particular deserve the accolade 'superlative'.

William Wordsworth was born in Cockermouth in 1770 and died at Rydal Mount in 1850. There are Wordsworth associations and houses all over the area, including Dove Cottage in Grasmere, Rydal Mount, Ullswater (which inspired Daffodils) and Grasmere Churchyard, where he is buried.

Beatrix Potter was born in London, in 1866, but became a frequent visitor to the Lake District during her teenage years. She created Peter Rabbit and her other wonderful characters, and published her first book in 1901. In 1905, she bought Hill Top Farm and became devoted to Lakeland life. When she died in 1943, she left her land to the National Trust.

Opposite: Skiddaw, Cumbria.

the well-preserved Hardknott Fort was re-built by Hadrian. However, Ravenglass was Agricola's largest venture in Cumbria; his fort and naval base were built in AD78 and housed about 1000 legionnaires. The fort's bath-house, known as Walls Castle, is one of the best preserved in the country with the highest standing Roman walls in the north of England.

Above: Ravenglass.

Hadrian

Hadrian created the greatest and longest Roman remain in Britain, his Wall. Its construction started in AD122 and it ran from Bowness on the Solway Firth to Newcastle, a distance of 118 km (74 miles). There are some interesting remains east of Carlisle (*see* Northumbria section for the full story).

Romanies

Appleby-in-Westmoreland is the site of one of the most colourful and spectacular events in Britain.

Since 1685, it has hosted the nation's largest Horse Fair every June. It attracts gypsies from all over the country, a gathering of horsemen, horse-drawn caravans and traditional gypsy skills and crafts that draws in many visitors.

Skiddaw .... 934 m (3054 ft)

Bow Fell .... 905 m (2960 ft)

Scafell Pike and Sca Fell are the most breathtaking, forming two separate peaks on a ridge overlooking Wast Water to the west and the Langdales to the east.

Helvellyn is the most photogenic. The summit is approached via narrow arêtes, most notably Striding Edge and Swirral Edge, and between the ridges are dry combes, such as Brown Cove, and a water-filled combe, Red Tarn.

Romans

Some of Cumbria's most famous visitors were Romans, including Agricola and Hadrian.

Agricola

Agricola was Governor of Britain during the Roman expansion northwards and he built roads and forts, including those linking Ambleside, Hardknott and Ravenglass.

Little remains of Galava Fort at Ambleside except its foundations, and

Nuclear Power

Cumbria has had a long association with the development of nuclear power in Britain.

The village of Seascale is the home of British Nuclear Fuels and, on 17 October, 1956, the first British nuclear power station started operating at Calder Hall. The complex now includes Sellafield, with its re-processing plant, which is one of the Lake District's most popular tourist attractions.

Visitors Welcome

The Sellafield Visitors' Centre explains the background of nuclear power, offers guided tours of the plant and Calder Hall and attracts over 130 000 visitors every year.

Left: Illustrations by Beatrix Potter.

Southern Scotland

From Churches and Castles to 'Rabbie' Burns and Gretna Green

This section covers the Borders and the area as far north as the Clyde–Forth line, but it excludes the great cities of Edinburgh and Glasgow which are covered separately.

The Borders are famous for the remains of abbeys, most of which were founded by David I. One of the greatest – and also the earliest – is Melrose. The Abbey's association with Robert the Bruce further enhances its position in history.

The west of the region contains the earliest Christian sites and the largest forest in Scotland.

Although the area was fought over during the centuries of border warfare between Scotland and England, the ensuing 200 years of peace have led to many of the castles and fortified towers being converted into stately residences with landscaped grounds, the finest of these being Culzean Castle and Traquair House.

The centre of the region contains some old industrial towns with interesting surprises, particularly Leadhills and Sanquar, whilst in the north of the area are the great Forth bridges.

The west of the region is literally littered with towns and villages claiming associations with Scotland 'national poet', Robert Burns, who was born at Alloway and died in Dumfries.

Last but certainly not least, the Blacksmith's Shop at Gretna Green must be the most romantic place in Britain.

Above: Bear Gates, Traquair House.

Close to the Abbey is the village of Newstead. It is sited on the foundations of the old Roman fort of Trimontium and has been occupied since AD200, making it the oldest continuously inhabited settlement in Scotland.

Ancient Christianity

Whithorn

St. Ninian established the first Christian settlement in Scotland. He arrived around 400 at Whithorn and established a church known as *Candida Casa*, the White House. Archaeological digs have revealed foundations from this period, although the present Priory dates from the 12th century.

Whithorn also has a rare collection of Christian memorials and crosses from the Dark Ages, including the Latinus Stone. Carved in the 5th century, it is the oldest Christian relic in Scotland.

Ruthwell

Further east up the Solway Firth is Ruthwell, the location of a 5.4 m (18 ft) high 7th-century cross. It is decorated with both Christian friezes and pagan runic symbols and is regarded as the greatest Dark-Age religious relic in Europe.

Historic Houses

Many buildings that were originally constructed as fortified strongholds have

Melrose

Melrose Abbey was founded by David I in 1136 and was the first Cistercian abbey in Scotland. Because of its position it was often ravaged during the border wars and the present remains date from 1385. The most magnificent of these is the stonework of the North Transept Window with its famous Crown of Thorns. Melrose was Robert the Bruce's favourite abbey, a fact clearly demonstrated in 1322 when, following Edward II's destruction of the Abbey the year before, he granted £2000 to rebuild and restore it. To put it into perspective, that amount was reputedly more money than was in the entire Scottish Treasury at the time! Legend also says that Robert the Bruce's heart is buried somewhere under the altar area at Melrose.

subsequently been developed as magnificent residences.

Culzean Castle

One of the greatest of these is Culzean Castle on the west coast. It was originally a medieval fortified tower-house, but was re-created by Robert Adams between 1772 and 1792 as a mansion surrounded by 226 ha (564 acres) of gardens.

In 1970, the quality of the gardens was officially recognised when they were named as Scotland's first Countryside Park. In 1990, the glories of Culzean attracted 365 679 visitors.

Traquair House

Traquair House, outside Peebles, is even more historic. A building was first erected there 1000 years ago and the buildings have been occupied continuously since then, making it the oldest continuously inhabited house in Scotland. Alexander I granted a charter to the owners in 1107, and over the centuries 27 Scottish and British monarchs have visited the House.

Below: Melrose Abbey.

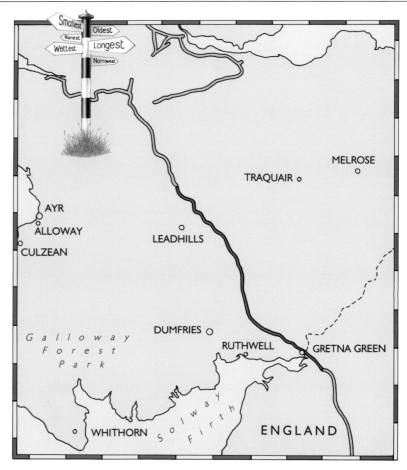

Mary Queen of Scots stayed at Traquair in 1566, as did Bonnie Prince Charlie in 1745. Charles Stuart visited whilst drumming up support for the campaign that took him to Derby and finally to defeat at Culloden. When he left, his cousin, the 5th Earl of Traquair, closed the great Bear Gates (the main gates to the House), declaring that they would never be opened again until a Stuart was on the throne of Scotland. They remain closed to this day.

Forestry

North of Whithorn the land rises towards Merrick, the highest point in southern Scotland at 842 m (2764 ft).

Merrick is part of the Galloway Forest Park which covers 35 275 ha (87 165 acres) and is the largest in Scotland and the second largest in Britain.

Bridging the Forth

By Rail

Edinburgh is on the south coast of the Firth of Forth and, as with the other great estuaries of Britain, access northwards was only possible after a lengthy detour inland to the first crossing point.

As per normal, this situation was not satisfactory for the Victorian railway engineers and so they decided to bridge the Forth just upstream from Edinburgh, at Queensferry. Work commenced in November 1882 and was finished in January 1890. The completed bridge carries a double railway track over the Forth, 47.5 m (156 ft) above the water level. At 521 m (1710 ft) long it is the longest cantilever bridge in Britain and the second longest in the world.

In 1990, to celebrate the Bridge's centenary, its entire length was floodlit, using 1000 high-powered sodium floodlights. More than 40 km (25 miles) of

Opposite: Scotland's most famous bridges.

Gretna Green

Gretna Green – and particularly its Blacksmith's Shop – has been famous since the mid-18th century. Changes in the marriage laws in England in 1754 outlawed secret marriages, but the law in Scotland required only that the would-be couple had witnesses, and Gretna was the first village north of the border. It became a mecca for eloping couples and remained one even when the law was changed, in 1856, forcing one half of the couple to live in Scotland for three weeks before the ceremony.

The Blacksmith's Shop has not been used for 'real' weddings since Scottish law was finally tightened up in 1940, but it still performs ceremonies for visitors and, in 1990, attracted more than 300 000 people.

Above: The Burns Monument, erected 1820.

the Forth as part of the A90/M90 Edinburgh-to-Perth road.

They built their suspension bridge alongside the rail bridge and it was completed in 1964. It has a total length of 1006 m (5979 ft) and is the longest suspension bridge in Scotland, second longest in Britain and eighth longest in the world.

Leadhills

Leadhills, as its name implies, was a centre for lead mining in Scotland in the 18th and 19th centuries.

In 1741, the town was endowed with a library by the poet Allan Ramsey, probably best known for his poem, *The Gentle Shepherd*. His Miners' Library is the oldest subscription library in Britain and contains many 18th-century volumes and records of the mining industry.

Sanquar

Sanquar is southwest of Leadhills and its history goes back to the 15th century.

It was an important centre for the Covenanters in the 17th century and a major coal-mining town until the 1960s. It is also the location of the oldest post office in Britain. The office was established in 1763 and ran a horse-ridden mail service to Edinburgh.

Robert Burns

Robert Burns lived for less than 37 years but his works have led to him being regarded as Scotland's 'National Poet'. There are memorials to him, and places linked with him, throughout the west of southern Scotland but three of the most famous are Alloway, Ayr and Dumfries.

Auld Kirk

Burns was born in Alloway on 25 January, 1759, and spent the first seven years of his life in a thatched cottage that has been preserved in memory of him. Alloway's Auld Kirk is the resting place of Burns' father and was one of the locations the poet used in *Tam O'Shanter*.

cabling was used whilst erecting the lights and the Forth Railway Bridge is now the largest illuminated bridge in the world. The lights will remain on until at least the year 2000.

By Road

The road engineers of the 1950s and '60s were, in their own way, as inventive and creative as the Victorian rail engineers, and they decided to bridge

The Burns Monument

Ayr can be reached from Alloway by crossing the famous Auld Brig o'Doon; alongside this is The Burns Monument, which was erected in 1820. Burns was baptised at Ayr's Auld Kirk and the town contains many celebrations of the poet.

Resting Place

He died in Dumfries on 21 July, 1796, having lived the last five years of his life in the city, working as an exciseman.

Above: Brig o'Doon.

There are again many Burns associations in the city – the house in which he died is now a Burns Museum and his remains are in the Burns Mausoleum.

Edinburgh and Glasgow

A Capital and a Commercial Centre

Edinburgh and Glasgow form a strange set of twins on the east and west coasts of Scotland separated by a mere 72 km (45 miles).

Neither city is particularly old. There are some signs of pre-historic settlements on the tops of the volcanic hills around Edinburgh but the city itself probably dates from the 8th or 9th century and may have been founded by Edwin, King of Northumbria, from which came 'Edwin's burgh'. The earliest buildings still in existence date from the early 12th century, and Edinburgh only became the official capital of Scotland in the mid-15th century.

Glasgow was founded around a church built by St. Mungo in the 6th century and was originally known as 'Gles Ghn' (the green place). The cathedral built on St. Mungo's site dates from 1197 and the oldest domestic building in Glasgow dates from 1471, although its University was founded in 1451, and a great deal of Glasgow dates from the Industrial Revolution and the Victorian era in particular.

Both cities contribute an enormous amount to the architectural, artistic and cultural life of Scotland.

Edinburgh – Athens of the North

Edinburgh has a population of just under 500 000 and is the second largest city in Scotland. The centre of the city is dominated by Edinburgh Castle which sits on Castle Rock, 82 m (270 ft) above the surrounding area.

Edinburgh Castle

Malcolm III defeated the kings of Northumbria and took possession of Edinburgh in 1018. He built a wooden fortress on top of the vantage point now known as Castle Rock, and his Saxon wife, Queen Margaret, persuaded him to use the town as his base rather than his preferred capital, Dunfermline. She also organised the building of a Christian chapel on the highest point of the Rock and died in what became known as St. Margaret's Chapel, in 1093.

A few years later, at the start of the 12th century, the Chapel was re-built in stone and, although restored over the centuries, it remains the oldest extant building in Edinburgh.

Edinburgh Castle has been fought over and destroyed on a number of occasions over the centuries, most notably when Robert the Bruce ordered the entire Castle, except for St. Margaret's Chapel, to be razed to the ground.

Mary Queen of Scots lived in the castle during 1566 when she gave birth to the future James VI, the last King of Scotland and first King of England *and* Scotland.

The present buildings date mainly from the 17th century and they successfully repulsed a siege by Bonnie Prince Charlie's forces in 1745.

Edinburgh Castle is most famous nowadays because of the annual Military Tattoo, one of the largest regular outdoor military displays in the world. In 1990, the Castle received 1 078 180 visi-

Left: Face-painting at the Festival.

tors, making it the most popular fee-charging tourist attraction in Scotland.

The Kirk and Parliament

The roads running northeast from Edinburgh Castle to the entrance to Holyroodhouse are known as 'The Royal Mile', although they are in reality a little bit more than a mile long. On either side of The Royal Mile are some of the most important buildings of royal and medieval Edinburgh.

The High Kirk of St. Giles stands on a site that has been used for worship since AD854. The first church was destroyed and St. Giles was re-founded in the 12th century, burnt by the English in 1385, re-built in 1390 and had its distinctive steeple added in 1495.

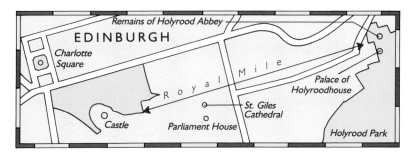

Alongside St. Giles is the Parliament House, the setting – in 1707 – of the signing of the Act of Union between England and Scotland. This Act signalled the end of Scotland as a separate nation and the dissolution of the Scottish Parliament. The minutes of the last meeting of Parliament stopped in mid-sentence when it became obvious to the clerks that Scotland was voting itself out of existence.

The Palace and Abbey

At the end of The Royal Mile is the Palace and Abbey of Holyroodhouse. The Abbey came first and was founded

Below: Parliament House, Edinburgh.

The Edinburgh Military Tattoo, part of the Festival.

in the 12th century by David I. Reputedly, he was hunting in the forests around Arthur's Seat in 1128, when he grappled with a stag and found a cross linking its antlers, which he decided to keep. Soon after, he had a dream that he must build an abbey to house the 'holy rood' (the cross).

The first Palace was built by James IV as a royal residence in the mid-15th century, when Edinburgh became the official capital of Scotland. Mary Queen of Scots lived there for six years and, following the Restoration, Charles II had the present Palace built by Sir William Bruce. It is still the Monarch's official residence in Scotland.

The New Town

Until the middle of the 18th century, Edinburgh's development was limited by the fact that the ridge that formed Castle Rock and ran down to Holyrood faced a shallow water, called the North Loch, with open fields beyond. In 1752, the then Lord Provost, George Drummond, began to develop a plan to bridge and fill the Loch and develop the fields.

The New Town, as it became known, was built under rigid controls and is still subject to stringent conservation and usage rules. Due to this, Edinburgh New Town is the greatest Georgian city in Scotland and Charlotte Square is particularly fine. Planned by Robert Adams in 1791, but built after his death, it is regarded as one of the greatest civic squares in Europe.

Libraries, Museums, Galleries and Gardens

As befits a capital city, Edinburgh is the home of Scotland's national collections, including the Scottish National Gallery, National Library, National Portrait Gallery, Royal Botanic Gardens and Royal Museum.

The National Library has developed from the Advocates' Library, which was founded in 1682 and is the oldest

Above: The present buildings of Edinburgh Castle.

library in Scotland. It is also the fourth largest library in Britain.

The Royal Botanic Gardens cover 28 ha (70 acres) and include the largest collection of rhododendrons in Britain. The Gardens moved to their present site in 1823 and are the most popular gardens in Scotland, having been visited by 785 591 people in 1990.

The Festival

The annual Edinburgh International Festival lasts for three weeks in late summer.

It was first held in 1947 and has grown to include the 'official' Festival; the famous 'Fringe', and film, television, book and jazz festivals. Even the Princes Street Firework Display and Edinburgh

Military Tattoo have been incorporated into the 'show' and it is the largest arts festival in the world.

Below: Festival buskers.

Glasgow – City of Culture

Glasgow has a population of nearly 800 000. It is the largest city in Scotland and the third largest in Britain.

The only completely medieval cathedral on the Scottish mainland can be found there, with a rich history, but most of the city's greatest buildings date from the 19th and 20th centuries.

The Cathedral

St. Mungo founded his church in Glasgow in AD543 but nothing remains of this and very little of the first Norman cathedral that was erected in 1136.

However, the present building is on the site of the first two and was started in 1197. It survived the Reformation with little damage, mainly thanks to the protection of the Glasgow Guilds, and because of this protection it shares with the cathedral at Kirkwall, in Orkney, the distinction of being the only Scottish cathedrals to have had their medieval structures preserved.

Its crypt is unusual in that it is not really underground because of the rising

Below: Provand's House.

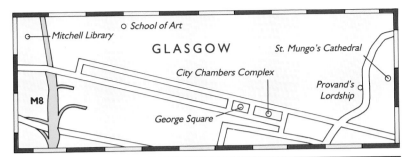

Above: Glasgow Cathedral.

ground the cathedral is built on. It is often called the Lower Church and is the finest Gothic vaulted crypt in Europe.

History

The oldest domestic building in Glasgow dates from 1471. It is called Provand's Lordship and was probably built as a dwelling for the Chaplain of the Cathedral's almshouse.

However, Glasgow was certainly well populated and important prior to this date. It was created a royal burgh in 1450 and, one year later, the University was founded.

The dawning of the industrial age and international trade saw Glasgow well placed. Located on the west coast of Scotland, it became important from the 1700s onwards, particularly after the Clyde was deepened to allow large ships into the Firth.

In the 18th century, Glasgow was often referred to as the 'second city of the

Above: Glasgow Chambers.

Empire' and its importance and prosperity was reflected in the scale of public building undertaken by the city fathers.

The power, wealth and confidence of the city in the 19th century culminated in George Square, which contains 12 major statues and Glasgow City Chambers. The Chambers were built between 1883 and 1888 in an Italianate style.

The Hunterian Museum was built in 1807 and is the oldest museum in Scotland.

The Mitchell Library was founded in 1874. It contains over 1 000 000 volumes (including the largest collection of works on Robert Burns in the world), and is the largest public reference library in Europe.

Re-development

The middle years of the 20th century saw Glasgow in decline, with ageing heavy industries and the legacies of under-investment and overcrowding, but the present city fathers have shown that they can rise to a challenge.

The re-development, re-building and restoration of the city caused a resurgence that led to it hosting the National Garden Festival in 1988, and becoming the official European City of Culture for 1990.

Mackintosh's Masterpieces

Charles Rennie Mackintosh was born in 1868 and, by the age of 22, he was winning scholarships and awards for his designs. He turned his Art Nouveau approach to designing everything from cutlery and furniture to entire buildings, and Glasgow is fortunate enough to hold some of his greatest works.

His masterpiece is undoubtedly the Glasgow School of Art. He won a competition to create the School's new building and it was erected between 1897 and 1907. The Willow Tea Rooms are another fine example of his work, and the Hunterian Art Gallery contains a complete reconstruction of his own house in Glasgow and its contents.

Mackintosh was certainly a great and gifted man, but he became a very disillusioned one. He eventually stopped working on his designs and retired to France to paint. He died there in 1928.

Scottish Highlands and Islands

From Magnificent Scenery and Ancient Remains to the Most Famous of Monsters

The Scottish Highlands and Islands cover a vast stretch of Britain northwards from the Clyde–Forth line. The area contains some of Britain's most spectacular mountain scenery, including all seven British mountains that are more than 1250 m (4100 ft) high.

The mountain ranges are cut by deep valleys and glens, and the largest and deepest of the Scottish lochs and lakes. Not to be outdone, the coastlines, particularly in the north of the mainland and on the islands, have some of Britain's greatest sea cliffs and awesome features, including the Old Man of Hoy.

The region, particularly Orkney and Shetland, also contains some of Europe's most remarkable remains of pre-historic man. The Highlands and Islands are littered with monuments to man's efforts to subdue the landscape and his fellow man.

From pre-historic times onwards, monuments include castles and forts and battle sites. There are also ancient religious sites, such as Iona, and educational centres, like St. Andrews, as well as the usual Victorian efforts to bring transport and trade.

Scotland is regarded as the birthplace and natural home of the game of golf, nowhere more so than St. Andrews.

The Highlands have more than their fair share of mysteries and legends, from Macbeth's witches to Robert the Bruce's spider, but none is more talked-about than Nessie, the elusive monster of Loch Ness.

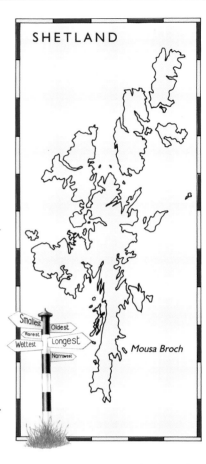

SHETLAND

Smallest · Oldest · Rarest · Wettest · Longest · Narrowest

Mousa Broch

The Land

The upland areas of the region include the Grampians, the Cairngorms and the Highlands and are made of the hardest and oldest rock formations in Britain. The Scourian rocks of the northwest Highlands include gneiss that has been metamorphosed from igneous rocks that were originally crystallised 2800 million years ago and are the oldest rocks in Britain.

The last Ice Age scoured and shaped the region's landscape, over-deepening the river valleys to create sites for the lochs, giving the mountains their characteristic rounded slopes and, on the highest mountains, leaving craggy, frost-shattered peaks. The last major ice sheets retreated from the region only around 10 000 years ago and the Highland landscape is still a very immature one with nature trying to adjust to the post-ice environment.

Ben Nevis

Ben Nevis is a relatively accessible mountain, being only 6.85 km (4¼ miles) southeast of the town of Fort William, which is connected by both road and rail to Glasgow. It is also the highest mountain in Britain, although it was not officially recognised as such until 1870. It rises to a height of 1343 m (4406 ft) and the top is surmounted by a 3.65 m (12 ft) tall cairn.

The climb from the Fort William direction is relatively easy; the real glory and

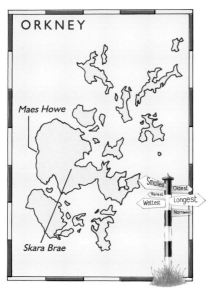

ORKNEY

Maes Howe

Smallest
Rarest Oldest
Wettest Longest
Narrowest

Skara Brae

mountaineering challenge of Ben Nevis is its north side with crags, gullies and spectacular 600 m (2000 ft) cliffs and rock faces.

The Water

Lochs

The over-deepening of the river valleys was most prominent in the Highlands. Loch Morar, west of Inverness, is the deepest lake in Britain, reaching an extreme depth of 310 m (1017 ft). Loch Ness, to the southwest of Inverness, has places almost as deep as this, reaching nearly 300 m (1000 ft) and has an average depth of 130 m (427 ft) along its enormous 38.99 km (24.23 mile) length, but more of Loch Ness later.

The largest lake in the whole of Britain is Loch Lomond in the southwest of the region. It is 36.44 km (22.64 miles) long, narrow and fjord-like in the north – rarely more than 1.6 km (1 mile) wide – and surrounded by mountains including, on its eastern shore, Ben Lomond which rises to 976 m (3192 ft).

It is deepest in the north, reaching an extreme depth of 190 m (623 ft). The southern half of the lake as it leaves the mountains is much broader and shallower, reaching 8 km (5 miles) wide and only 23 m (75 ft) deep.

Loch Lomond covers a total area of 70.04 km² (27.45 sq. miles) and con-

Below: Ben Nevis.

tains 30 islands, including Inchmurrin which, with an area of 115 ha (284 acres), is the largest island in a lake in Britain.

Waterfalls

Part of the adjustment of the landscape to its post-Ice-Age environment means that the over-deepening of the valleys has left tributary valleys 'lost' high on the mountain sides, and the streams in these valleys fall to the main valley in spectacular waterfalls, until they can cut back their own courses to reach the valley floor at the correct level.

The region has many waterfalls, the most spectacular being Eas a Chual Aluinn in Sutherland, which falls 200 m (568 ft) and is the highest waterfall in Britain.

Cliffs

When the mountains reach the shores around the north of the region, and particularly on the islands, they often fall sheerly into the sea creating magnificent cliffs. The raging northern seas batter these hard rocks and have created some amazing seascapes.

The cliffs on the island of St. Kilda are the highest in Britain, and at Conachair they reach a height of 396 m (1300 ft). The cliffs of Sutherland are also spectacular – at Cape Wrath they reach 281 m (921 ft), making them the highest cliffs on the British mainland.

Of all of the features carved into the cliffs by the eroding sea, the most impressive is the Old Man of Hoy on the island of Hoy, part of Orkney. The Old Man is Britain's tallest sea stack, an isolated pillar of rock cut off from the cliff face by the sea. It rises steeply for 137 m (450 ft) and was not climbed until 1966.

Orkney and Shetland

Orkney and Shetland are two distinct groups of islands northeast of Scotland.

Orkney is the closest group with the southernmost islands, Hoy and South Ronaldsay, only 10 km (6 miles) from the Scottish coast. Orkney consists of 70 islands, the largest of which is called Mainland.

Shetland is much more isolated. The southern tip of its largest island, which is also called Mainland, is 176 km (110 miles) northeast of Scotland and its northern islands are closer to the Norwegian city of Bergen than they are to Britain.

There are more than 100 islands forming the Shetland group, although only 14 are inhabited, including Fair Isle. Fair Isle is part of Shetland but is midway between the two island groups – 53 km (33 miles) from the closest point of the rest of Shetland and 43 km (27 miles) from the closest point on Orkney. It is the most isolated settlement in Britain.

The island groups, particularly Shetland, have more affinity to northern Europe than to the rest of the country. Shetland has been ruled by both Norway and Denmark and was only ceded to the Scottish throne in 1469.

Pre-history

Both Orkney and Shetland have some of the most spectacular remains of prehistoric man in Europe. The best of these are Maes Howe, Mousa Broch and Skara Brae.

Maes Howe in Orkney was built around 2500BC as the burial chamber of a powerful warrior and his family. It is the finest burial chamber in Europe. The 35 m (115 ft) diameter mound covers a vaulted stone chamber that is a 4.25 m (14 ft) square. Unfortunately, the graves were plundered in the 12th century and

Below: Loch Lomond – Scotland's largest lake.

Skara Brae contains spectacular prehistoric remains.

the contents were seized by the Vikings.

Mousa Broch in Shetland is the best-preserved broch in Britain. (A broch is an iron-age stone tower – its use was uncertain but it could have been a watch tower or defensive retreat).

Mousa Broch was built around 1BC and its remains are more than 12 m (40 ft) high with walls measuring 3.6 m (12 ft). The inside of the broch includes alcoves dug into the walls and, from the first floor upwards, a stone staircase.

Skara Brae in Orkney is unique in Britain and is one of the greatest stone-age sites in Europe. It is sometimes referred to as the 'Pompeii of Britain' and was established around 3000BC as a thriving Stone Age village. By 2600BC, it consisted of seven or eight huts which were linked by covered passages and supported a community of around 30 stone-age farmers.

One day, the village was literally engulfed by a huge sandstorm which covered everything. Skara Brae remained buried by a huge amount of sand and was left totally undisturbed for more than 4400 years, until it was discovered in 1850. Its subsequent excavation and exploration has provided us with a unique 'snapshot' of day-to-day life in a stone-age village. The site has revealed beds, cupboards and dressers, all made of stone, as well as tools, pottery and jewellery.

Iona

Iona is a small island off the southwest shore of Mull. St. Columba and 12 followers landed there in AD563 with the aim of converting the Scottish people to Christianity. They founded a monastery on the island but the present cathedral dates from the 15th century.

Malcolm III's wife, Margaret, is believed to have built a church on the site, or re-built St. Columba's original monastery, in the middle of the 11th cen-

Above: An Atholl Highlander, Blair Castle.

tury, but between 1098 and 1266 the church was part of the Norwegian archdiocese of Trondheim and it was only given cathedral status in 1507, when it became the base of the Bishop of the Isles. It was dissolved in 1561 and has subsequently been restored on a number of occasions, most recently between 1902 and 1910 and is now the home of the Iona Community.

St. Columba's Cell was probably on Tor Abb, to the west of the Cathedral. Outside the Cathedral there are three famous 9th-century Celtic Christian crosses – of St. Matthew, St. Martin and St. John. The Cathedral's burial ground gives a clear indication of the religious significance of Iona as it contains the graves of 48 Scottish kings, four Irish kings and eight Norwegian kings.

Blair Atholl and Pitlochry

Blair Castle at Blair Atholl was founded in 1270 and is the home of the Duke of Atholl. In 1745, the then Duke supported Bonnie Prince Charlie and lent him the Castle. Following the Prince's defeat at Culloden, it was occupied by the Duke of Cumberland's forces and so the Duke of Atholl besieged his own Castle in an attempt to regain control. The siege failed and it was the last attempted seizure of a castle to take place on British soil.

The Duke of Atholl is unique in Europe in that he has the only legal private army. The Atholl Highlanders are the Duke's own force, a privilege granted to the then Duke by Queen Victoria.

Nearby Pitlochry is the home of the famous Festival Theatre, the so-called 'Theatre in the Hills'. Close by is the Edradour Distillery, the smallest whisky distillery in Scotland, and the Pitlochry Power Station Fish Ladder. The Fish Ladder is a unique series of fish pools built up the side of the Power Station's dam to allow salmon to travel upstream to breed. They can be seen leaping from one pool to the next as they make their way to the top.

Dundee

Tay Bridge

Dundee is at the mouth of the River Tay, Scotland's longest river, which flows for 188 km (117 miles).

On the outskirts of the town is the Tay Railway Bridge, the longest railway bridge in Europe. It is a multiple-arch bridge with 85 arches, 74 of which are over water, and is 3552 m (11 653 ft) long.

The Bridge was opened on 20 June, 1887, to replace the ill-fated first Tay Bridge which collapsed when hit by a tornado during a storm on 28 December, 1879, killing all 75 people onboard the train that was crossing the bridge at the time.

Famous Ships

Dundee Harbour is the home of two famous ships. HMS *Unicorn* is the oldest British warship still afloat – the 46-gun, 46 m (152 ft) long frigate was launched in 1824. RRS *Discovery* was built in Dundee and is most famous as the mother ship for Captain Scott's last expedition to the South Pole (1901–4).

Dunfermline

Dunfermline was the capital of Scotland for 600 years and is the burial place of seven Scottish kings, including Robert the Bruce. Dunfermline Abbey was founded by Margaret, wife of Malcolm III, in 1072, and was the first of the great Norman Abbeys in Scotland.

Carnegie

However, Dunfermline's greatest claim to fame is that it was the birthplace of Andrew Carnegie, in 1835. In 1848, Carnegie and his family left for America where he made his enormous fortune, ninety per-cent of which he used for charitable deeds. Amongst other things, he founded 3000 Carnegie libraries around the world – the first of these was in his home town of Dunfermline, and was founded in 1881.

Inverness

Inverness is often called the 'Capital of the Highlands'. The Town Hall was the location of the first ever meeting of the British government cabinet to take place outside London.

Prime Minister Lloyd George was on holiday in Scotland in 1921 when it became essential for the cabinet to meet to discuss Irish independence. Rather than returning to London, he took the unusual of step of summoning his colleagues to Inverness to join him.

Nessie – Fact or Fiction?

Loch Ness runs along the line of the Great Glen Fault to the southwest of Inverness. It has an average depth of 130 m (427 ft) with deeps reaching almost 300 m (1000 ft). At 37.44 km (22.64 miles) it is the longest lake in Britain. Because of this combination it holds the greatest volume of water of any lake in Britain – 7 443 000 000 m³ (262 845 000 000 cu. ft). Plenty of room to hide anything!

The great depth of the Loch means that it never freezes and due to the surrounding peat moors the waters are dark and often impenetrable. Because the Great Glen Fault cuts Scotland in two between the Atlantic and the North Sea, it is feasible that at times of higher sea level the Loch was joined to the sea. It is also possible that there are still underwater channels linking the Loch with open water.

Exactly when the story of the Loch Ness Monster started is unclear, but over the past hundred years there have been many claims of sightings. Scientists have discussed the possibility of a family of aquatic dinosaurs surviving and breeding for millions of years in the hidden depths of the Loch, whilst hoaxers have used up-turned boats and tubing to product photographic 'evidence', and hi-tech expeditions have spent millions of pounds on laser and sonar soundings without proving or disproving anything.

More than 350 000 people a year visit the Official Loch Ness Monster Exhibition, so go and make up your own mind – stand in the romantic ruins of Urquhart Castle and peer over the mist-shrouded Loch whilst sipping a glass of fine malt whisky – you never know!

Culloden

Just east of Inverness is Culloden, the site of the last true battle on British soil. It was Scotland's last attempt to gain independence and the final attempt by the Stuarts to regain the throne.

On 16 April, 1746, Charles Stuart, 'Bonnie Prince Charlie', led 5000 Scottish clansmen against 9000 British troops controlled by George II's son, the Duke of Cumberland. The Battle of Culloden was a rout lasting only around 40 minutes, during which time the British troops killed 1000 Scottish soldiers whilst losing 50 of their own and leaving 250 wounded.

St. Andrews

St. Andrews is an ancient city with the remains of a mighty cathedral and castle. It is also the home of Scotland's oldest university, founded in 1411. Inspite of this history the name of St. Andrews means one thing throughout the world – golf.

'Royal and Ancient'

Golf has been played around the St. Andrews area since the 15th century and a course was laid out on the site of the present Old Course during the same

Opposite: RRS Discovery.

century. The first formal club, the Society of St. Andrews Golfers, was founded in 1764, although this was not the first golfing society in Scotland, and in 1834, William III conferred the title 'Royal and Ancient' on the Society.

Rules and Regulations

Towards the end of the 19th century, golf was becoming a very popular sport throughout Britain and the world, but

Above: St. Andrew's.

societies and clubs often devised their own rules. If the game was to continue to flourish, a standard set of rules had to be devised. St. Andrews Royal and Ancient Society were invited to draw up a rule book in 1897 and the *R & A Rule Book* has controlled the game ever since.

Below: Culloden – site of the 40-minute rout.

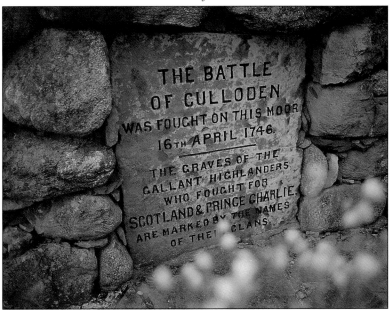

Northern Ireland

From Water to Whiskey and a Very Fine Umbrella

Northern Ireland is a distinctive part of the United Kingdom and no guide to what are effectively the superlatives of the *whole* of Britain would be complete without the inclusion of natural features such as Lough Neagh or the Giant's Causeway. Nor would the gazetteer be complete without the inclusion of industrial superlatives, such as the Harland and Wolff Shipyard and the mighty cranes, Samson and Goliath.

Here then are some of Northern Ireland's superlatives, including the world's oldest distillery and one of the world's most distinctive and most-photographed shop signs.

Above: The Holestone, Co. Antrim.

Up in County Antrim, in the town of Bushmills, the distillery uses water from the same source it has used for centuries. The Old Bushmills Distillery was first licensed in 1608, making it the oldest licensed spirit producer in the world, although the distillery is claimed to have been producing whiskey as early as 1276.

The Giant's Causeway

On the Antrim Coast close to Bushmills is one of the world's greatest natural wonders – the Giant's Causeway.

At this World Heritage Site there are almost 40 000 massive basalt columns. The basalt intruded into the surrounding chalk around 60 000 000 years ago and cooled and solidified slowly, crystallising into huge polygonal columns, mainly hexagonal. The longest columns are around 12 m (40 ft) high.

Finn MacCool

It is called the Giant's Causeway because legend has it that the famous giant, Finn MacCool, decided that he wanted to travel from Ireland to Scotland without getting his feet wet and built a great road to link the two countries.

Opposite: The Giant's Causeway.

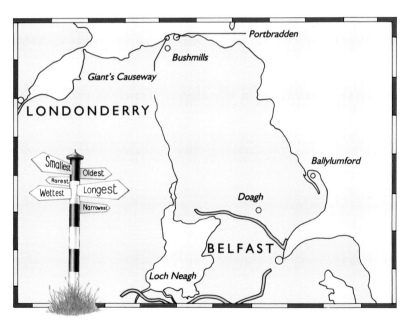

Lough Neagh

Lough Neagh is the largest freshwater lake in the UK. It covers an area of 381.73 km² (147.39 sq. miles) and is 28.9 km (18 miles) long and 17.7 km (11 miles) wide. It has a maximum depth of 31 m (102 ft) and was formed approximately 20 000 years ago from melting glaciers at the end of the last Ice Age. Eight rivers flow into Lough Neagh but only one flows out.

Whiskey and Water

Water is an essential ingredient in one of Ireland's greatest products, *uisce beatha* – whiskey.

Over the centuries the sea has destroyed Finn MacCool's causeway and only the two landward ends can still be seen, in Scotland at Fingal's Cave on the Isle of Staffa and, most spectacularly, in Ireland at the Giant's Causeway.

St. Gobhan's

Also on the Antrim Coast, at Portbraddan, is St. Gobhan's Church. Although no t in regular public use, it is a family chapel and is used for worship by visiting youth holiday groups. It is the smallest church in Ireland and one of the smallest in the world, measuring only 3.7 m (12 ft) by 2 m (6 ft).

Below: St. Gobhan's Church.

Ancient Monuments

There are many monuments to ancient man in Northern Ireland and two in particular deserve a mention here.

'Holey' Matrimony

The Holestone is on a hilltop near Doagh in County Antrim. It was erected during the Bronze Age, and the 1.5 m (5 ft) tall megalith has a small hole cut through the centre of it, a hole too small for a man's hand to fit into but just large enough for a woman's.

The Holestone is Ireland's only betrothal monument and couples wishing to be married used to plight their troth by clasping hands through the Holestone.

Johnson's Umbrella

Belfast is Northern Ireland's capital, largest population and industrial core, and an important centre for culture, entertainment and shopping.

Johnson's in Ann Street is a famous umbrella shop in the city centre. In 1958 the owners decided that they should create a new shop sign to leave passers-by in no doubt about what the shop was selling. They commissioned an artist to create a sleeved male arm and hand holding a gold umbrella, extending from the front wall of their shop. Thirty-five years later, Johnson's Umbrella is still there and is one of the most distinctive shop signs in the world — and one of the most photographed.

An Inconvenient Monument

The second ancient monument is popularly known as 'Ireland's Most Inconvenient Neolithic Monument'. The Ballylumford Dolmen on Islandmagee, near Larne in County Antrim, is a most spectacular Neolithic dolmen with the capstone preserved in position. It is also known as the Druid's Altar. The problem is that it is in the small front garden of an occupied house, stops daylight from entering the front of the house and forces the occupants to gain access via a side door!

THE GUINNESS BOOK OF

BRITAIN

Records, Facts and Feats

THE GAZETTEER

Macclesfield Canal, Cheshire.

Natural WORLD

Oldest rock formation

Scourian gneisses in the Scottish North West Highlands dated at 2 800 000 000 years old.

Highest/lowest temperatures

Highest Cheltenham [Heart of England], on 3 August 1990, 37.1°C [100.5° F].

Lowest Braemar [Scottish Highlands and Islands], on 10 January 1982, −27.2°C [−17° F].

Rainfall

Highest annual Sprinkling Tarn [Cumbria], 1954, 6527 mm [257 in].

Below: the Royal Botanic Gardens, Edinburgh – second in the visitors league.

Top ten gardens

Kew Gardens [London]	1 196 000
Royal Botanic Gardens [Edinburgh]	786 000
Walsall Arboretum [North West]	450 000
Oxford University Botanic Gardens [T & C]	400 000
Belfast Botanic Gardens [Northern Ireland]	350 000
Glasgow Botanic Gardens [Glasgow]	350 000
Dixon Park, Belfast [Northern Ireland]	300 000
Stourhead [West Country]	228 000
Bodnant Gardens [North Wales]	170 000
Sissinghurst Castle Gardens [South East]	170 000

Highest monthly Llyn Llydau [North Wales], October 1909, 1436 mm [56.54 in].

Highest daily Martinstown, Dorset [West Country], 19 July 1955, 279 mm [11 in].

Lowest annual Margate, Kent [South East England], 1921, 236 mm [9.29 in].

Snowfall

Highest annual Upper Teesdale [North-umbria] and Denbighshire Hills [North Wales], 1947, 1524 mm [60 in].

Hailstones

Heaviest Horsham [Southern England], 5 September 1958, 141 gm [5 oz].

Droughts

Longest Mile End [London], 73 days between 4 March and 15 May 1893.

Frosts

Longest Great Dun Fell [Cumbria], 40 days from 23 January to 3 March 1986.

Shortest Bishop Rock, Isles of Scilly [The South West], during the entire period of scientific records the temperature has never fallen below 1°C [34°F].

Mountain peaks

Highest in Britain Ben Nevis, Fort William [Scottish Highlands and Islands], 1343 m [4406 ft].

Highest in Wales Snowdon [North Wales], 1085 m [3560 ft].

Highest in England Scafell Pike [Cumbria], 977 m [3206 ft].

Highest in Northern Ireland Slieve Donard, 852 m [2796 ft].

Below: Mount Snowdon – the highest mountain in Wales.

Top ten wildlife locations

London Zoo [London] *1 250 000*
Windsor Safari Park [Thames and Chilterns] *1 050 000*
Chester Zoo [North West] *1 000 000*
Leeds Tropical World [Yorks and Humberside] *863 000*
Edinburgh Zoo [Edinburgh] *542 000*
Whipsnade Park [Thames and Chilterns] *530 000*
Lotherton Bird Garden [Yorks and Humberside] *490 000*
Twycross Zoo [Heart of England] *462 000*
Bristol Zoo [West Country] *450 000*
Cotswold Wildlife Park [West Country] *376 000*

Depressions

Lowest Holme Fen, Cambridgeshire [East Anglia], 2.79 m [9 ft] below sea level.

Rivers

Longest in Britain Severn, 354 km [220 miles].

Longest wholly in England Thames, 346 km [215 miles].

Longest wholly in Scotland Tay, 188 km [117 miles].

Longest wholly in Wales Usk, 104 km [65 miles].

Lakes

Largest in Britain Lough Neagh [Northern Ireland], surface area of 381.73 km² [147.38 sq. miles].

Northern Ireland

● *LARGEST LAKE – Lough Neagh – 381.73 km² [147.38 sq. miles]*

Largest in Scotland Loch Lomond [Scottish Highlands and Islands], 36.44 km [22.64 miles] long with a surface area of 70.04 km² [27.45 sq. miles]

Opposite: Edinburgh Zoo.

Largest in England Windermere [Cumbria] measuring 16.8 km [10.5 miles] long, 1.47 km [1610 yards] wide, 66 m [219 ft] deep and covering 14.7 km² [5.69 sq. miles].

Largest volume (man-made) Kielder Water [Northumbria], contains 2 000 000 000 hl [44 000 000 000 gallons] in a lake with a perimeter of 43.4 km [27 miles] and a surface area of 10.85 km² [4.19 sq. miles], the largest in Europe.

Largest area (man-made) Rutland Water [East Midlands], total surface area of 12.54 km² [4.84 sq. miles], the largest in Europe.

Longest in Britain Loch Ness [Scottish Highlands and Islands], 38.99 km [24.23 miles] long.

Deepest in Scotland Loch Morar [Scottish Highlands and Islands], extreme depth of 310 m [1.017 ft].

Deepest in England Wast Water [Cumbria], 78 m [258 ft] deep.

Highest in Britain Lochan Buidhe [Scottish Highlands and Islands], 1097 m [3600 ft] above sea level.

Highest in England Bread Crag Tarn, Scafell Pike [Cumbria], 837 m [2748 ft] above sea level.

LANDSCAPE FEATURES

Bars and spits

Longest bar Chesil Beach, Dorset [West Country], 16 km [10 miles] long and between 180 m [600 ft] and 900 m [3000 ft] wide linking Abbotsbury and Portland.

Below: Lake Windermere, Cumbria.

Cliffs

Tallest Conachair, St. Kilda [Scottish Highlands and Islands], 396 m [1300 ft] high.

Coves

Archetypal Lulworth Cove, Dorset [West Country], the 'textbook cove'.

Islands

Largest Britain – surface area 218 040 km² [84 186 sq. miles], the eighth largest island in the world.

Northern Ireland is part of the island of Ireland, surface area 82 462 km² [31 834 sq. miles], the 20th largest island in the world.

Largest off-shore island Lewis with Harris [Scottish Highlands and Islands], 2225 km² [859 sq. miles].

Waterfalls

Longest in Britain Eas a Chual Aluinn, Sutherland [Scottish Highlands and Islands], 200 m [568 ft].

Longest in England Gaping Gill, Ingleborough Cave System, Yorkshire Dales [Yorkshire and Humberside], 111 m [365 ft].

Longest in England – above ground Scale Force [Cumbria], 45 m [148 ft].

Longest in Wales Pistyll-y-Llyn [Mid Wales], 90 m [300 ft].

Longest in Northern Ireland River Burntollet, 12 m [39 ft].

Biggest flow High Force [Northumbria].

Most visited Swallow Falls, Betws-y-coed [North Wales], 200 000 visitors in 1990.

Gorges

Largest Cheddar Gorge, Somerset [West Country]. Deepest point is 150 m [500 ft] from the surrounding hills to the floor of the gorge.

The West Country

- LONGEST SEA BAR – Chesil Beach in Dorset – 15 km [10 miles] long
- LARGEST GORGE – Cheddar Gorge in Somerset
- OLDEST THEATRE – Theatre Royal, Bristol – 1766
- TALLEST LIGHTHOUSE – Bishops Rock in the Isles of Scilly – 47.8 m [156.8 ft]
- LARGEST MAZE – At Longleat House near Warminster

The magnificent Cheddar Gorge, Somerset.

Burke and Hare, Madame Tussaud's.

National parks

First Peak District [East Midlands], created 17 April 1951, covering 1404 km² [524 sq. miles].

Most recent Brecon Beacons [South Wales], covering 1344 km² [519 sq. miles], created in 1967.

Largest Lake District [Cumbria], covering 2292 km² [885 sq. miles], created in 1951.

Smallest in Britain Pembrokeshire Coast [South Wales], 583 km² [225 sq. miles], created in 1952.

Smallest in England Exmoor [The South West], 686 km² [265 sq. miles], created in 1954.

WILDLIFE

Birds

Largest reserve Slimbridge, Gloucestershire [Heart of England], founded by Sir Peter Scott in 1946; 38 ha [94 acres], home to 3300 birds from 164 species including 400 flamingos, also a 323 ha [800 acres] refuge for migrating wildfowl.

Largest swannery The Abbotsbury Swannery, Abbotsbury, Dorset [West Country], founded in the 14th century – 500 swans.

Caves

Largest system Ease Gill System, Whernside, Yorkshire Dales [Yorkshire and Humberside], 66 km [41 miles] of caverns and passages.

Largest entrance Peak Cavern, Castleton [East Midlands], entrance 10 m [33 ft] high and 30 m [100 ft] wide.

FORESTS AND NATURAL LANDSCAPES

Forests

Largest in Britain Kielder Forest [Northumbria], 393.68 km² [152 sq. miles], largest artificially-planted forest in Europe.

Largest in Wales Coed Morgannwg [South Wales], 17 845 ha [44 095 acres].

Largest in Scotland Galloway Forest Park [Southern Scotland], 35 275 ha [87 165 acres].

Areas of outstanding beauty

First designated The Gower Peninsular [South Wales] in 1956.

Top ten leisure attractions

Blackpool Pleasure Beach [North West]	6 500 000
Liverpool Albert Docks [North West]	6 000 000
Strathclyde Park [Southern Scotland]	4 200 000
Brighton Palace Pier [South East]	3 500 000
Yarmouth Pleasure Beach [East Anglia]	2 600 000
Madame Tussaud's [London]	2 547 000
Alton Towers [Heart of England]	2 070 000
Chessington Adventures [South East]	1 515 000
Southport Pleasure World [North West]	1 500 000
Blackpool Tower [North West]	1 426 000

Superlative SUPERLATIVES

BRITAIN'S WORLD BEATERS

Amongst our nation's superlatives are the following world record holders:

THE SMALLEST CATHEDRAL CITY – St. David's, South Wales

THE LARGEST NORMAN CRYPT – Canterbury Cathedral, Kent

THE HEAVIEST PEAL OF BELLS – Liverpool Cathedral

THE OLDEST METHODIST CHAPEL – New Room, Bristol

Above: Liverpool Cathedral.

Above: Windsor Castle.

THE LARGEST INHABITED CASTLE – Windsor Castle

THE OLDEST CARNEGIE LIBRARY – Dunfermline, Scotland

THE LARGEST ARTS FESTIVAL – The Edinburgh Festival

THE LARGEST SOUND STAGE – Pinewood Studios

THE LONGEST SEASIDE PIER – Southend-on-Sea, Essex

THE SMALLEST BARBER'S SHOP – Palace Pier, Brighton

THE OLDEST MODEL VILLAGE – Beckonscot, Beaconsfield, Buckinghamshire

THE LARGEST CAMERA OBSCURA – Aberystwyth, Mid Wales

THE OLDEST PUBLIC ZOO – The Zoological Society, London

THE OLDEST POT PLANT – Kew Gardens, London

THE OLDEST LICENSED DISTILLERY – Bushmills, Northern Ireland

THE LARGEST TURKEY FARM – Bernard Matthews, Norfolk

THE LONGEST SUSPENSION BRIDGE – *The Humber Road Bridge*

THE LARGEST ILLUMINATED BRIDGE – *The Forth Rail Bridge*

THE FIRST IRON BRIDGE – *Ironbridge, Telford*

THE FIRST RAILWAY STATION – *Liverpool Road Station, Manchester*

THE OLDEST PASSENGER RAILWAY COACHES – *Talyllyn Railway, Mid Wales.*

THE FIRST UNDERGROUND RAILWAY – *The London Underground*

THE OLDEST COMMISSIONED SHIP – HMS *Victory, Portsmouth*

THE OLDEST IRON-HULLED WARSHIP – HMS *Warrior, Portsmouth*

THE OLDEST IRON-HULLED, SCREW-DRIVEN SHIP – SS Great Britain, *Bristol*

THE BUSIEST INTERNATIONAL AIRPORT – *London Heathrow*

THE LARGEST MOVABLE BARRIER – *The Thames Barrier*

THE LARGEST BRICKWORKS – *London Brick Company, Bedfordshire*

THE LONGEST SHOPPING MALL – *Milton Keynes, Buckinghamshire*

THE LARGEST MENSWEAR SHOP – *Slater Menswear, Glasgow*

THE LARGEST TOYSHOP – *Hamleys, London*

THE LARGEST BOOKSHOP – *Foyles, London*

THE LARGEST RECORD SHOP – *The HMV Shop, London*

THE LARGEST FISH AND CHIP SHOP – *Harry Ramsden's in Guiseley*

Below: HMS *Warrior, Portsmouth.*

Human
WORLD

Earliest remains

In Britain Hoxne near Eye, Suffolk [East Anglia], 12 small stone clusters with associated broken bones and charcoal, dated at around 250 000BC.

Oldest structure Jura [Scottish Highlands and Islands], three stone circles dated at around 6000BC.

Burial chambers

Longest West Kennett Long Barrow, Wiltshire [Southern England]. Constructed around 2000BC this chambered tomb contained 30 bodies and is 106 m [350 ft] long, one of the longest in Europe.

Highest in England Five Wells, Taddington Moor [East Midlands], 427 m [1400 ft] above sea level, dated at 2000BC.

Best preserved Maes Howe, Orkney [Scottish Highlands and Islands], built around 2500BC, a 35 m [115 ft] diameter mound covering a vaulted stone

Most popular historic building, the Tower of London.

chamber 4.25 m [14 ft] square, regarded as the finest burial chamber in Europe.

Stone circles

Largest Avebury, Wiltshire [Southern England], complex structure of two circles both surrounded by an outer circle of 98 sarcen blocks and a 9 m [30 ft] deep ditch, covering a total area of 11.5 ha [29H acres], constructed by Neolithic farmers and in use for around 500 years from 2600BC.

Largest trilithons Stonehenge, Wiltshire [Southern England]. The five trilithons inside the stone circle are made of sarsen blocks each weighing around 50 tons – the total structure, which includes a ditch and ceremonial avenue, was built and used over a period of 1700 years from 2800BC onwards, with the main circle and trilithons being constructed around 2100BC. Its exact purpose is still unclear but it was obviously of great significance to Neolithic man and it is estimated that more than 30 million man-years were expended in its construction.

Mounds

Largest Silbury Hill, Wiltshire [Southern England], constructed around

Top ten historic buildings

Tower of London [London]	2 298 000
Edinburgh Castle [Edinburgh]	1 078 000
Bath Roman Baths [West Country]	950 000
Windsor Castle [Thames and Chilterns]	855 000
Stonehenge [West Country]	703 000
Warwick Castle [Heart of England]	685 000
Leeds Castle [South East]	540 000
Tower Bridge [London]	528 000
Hampton Court Palace [London]	525 000
Blenheim Palace [Thames and Chilterns]	517 000

2700BC, covering an area of 2.2 ha [5.4 acres] and rising to a height of 40 m [130 ft], the largest artificial mound in Europe.

Villages

Best preserved Skara Brae, Orkney [Scottish Highlands and Islands], stone-age village with huts and covered passageways, founded around 3000BC and buried by a sandstorm around 2600BC, totally covered and undisturbed until 1850; remains include details of beds, cupboards, tools, pottery and jewellery, unique in Britain, one of the greatest stone-age sites in Europe.

Fortifications

Broch Mousa Broch, Shetland [Scottish Highlands and Islands], iron-age stone *Mystical Stonehenge.*

tower built around 1BC, remains are 12 m [40 ft] high with walls 3.6 m [12 ft] thick.

Largest hill fort Maiden Castle near Dorchester, Dorset [West Country], a fortified stronghold occupied during both the Stone Age and Iron Age, a complex structure of ditches and ram-

Southern England

- **LARGEST STONE CIRCLE** – *Avebury in Wiltshire –* 11.5 ha [28½ acres]

- **LARGEST TRILITHONS** – *Stonehenge in Wiltshire*

- **TALLEST SPIRE** – *Salisbury Cathedral* – 122.7 m [404 ft]

- **OLDEST CLOCK** – *Salisbury Cathedral* – 1386

- **OLDEST WARSHIP** – *The* Mary Rose *at Portsmouth* – 1545

Britain's tallest spire – Salisbury Cathedral.

parts covering 50 ha [124 acres]. It was the headquarters of the Durotriges tribe until it was captured by Roman legions in AD44.

Highest iron-age Fort Ingleborough Hill, Yorkshire Dales [Yorkshire and Humberside], 724 m [2373 ft] high.

Hill figures

Oldest man Cerne Abbas Giant, Cerne Abbas, Dorset [West Country]. A rampant and warlike creature 55 m [180 ft] tall, thought to be a figure of Hercules carrying a 37 m [120 ft] long club, age

uncertain but probably first cut during the Roman occupation around AD190.

Oldest horse Uffington White Horse, Uffington, Oxfordshire [Thames and Chilterns], 114 m [374 ft] from nose to tail, probably first cut by iron-age man around 150BC.

Largest man Longman Man of Wilmington, Wilmington, East Sussex [South East England], 68 m [226 ft] tall.

Roman palaces

Largest Fishbourne Palace near Chichester, Sussex [South East England], built AD50, occupied until about AD280, rediscovered in 1960; formal palace with four wings and elaborate gardens, probably built for Cogidubnus, King of the Regni, a key supporter of the Roman forces; largest Roman buildings so far discovered in Britain.

Roman baths

Best preserved The Great Bath, Bath, Avon [West Country], 1st-century-AD bath house and temple built around hot mineral springs, re-discovered in the 18th century.

Roman amphitheatres

Largest in Britain Deva, Chester [North West England].

Largest in Wales Caerleon [South Wales], part of AD75 barracks of 2nd Legion.

Roman theatres

Largest St. Albans [Thames and Chilterns], 6000-seat stadium with stage at one end, the only Roman theatre in Britain.

Roman walls

Longest Hadrian's Wall [Northumbria/ Cumbria], built AD122, 122 km [76 miles] long, the greatest Roman remain in Britain.

Opposite: the Long Man, Wilmington.

Roman forts

Best preserved Housesteads, Hadrian's Wall [Northumbria], walls 186 m [610 ft] by 111 m [367 ft] enclosing remains of headquarters, troops' billets, latrines and granaries.

Best preserved walls Porchester Castle near Portsmouth [Southern England], a Saxon shore fort constructed in the 3rd century AD, remains of the walls are 5.5 m [18 ft] high and 3 m [10 ft] thick and are the best preserved Roman fortress walls in northern Europe.

Other Roman remains

Gateway Newport Arch, Lincoln [East Midlands], only complete gateway preserved in Britain.

Lighthouse Pharos, Dover Castle, Dover [South East England], originally a 24.5 m [80 ft] high tower topped by a beacon to guide shipping into the Roman harbour. The first 12 m [40 ft] are still standing – the tallest and oldest Roman remain in Britain.

Mosaic Woodchester, Gloucestershire [Heart of England]. The Woodchester Pavement was created around AD325 and the 1 600 000 individual tesserae cover an area of 14.3 m² [47 sq. ft], the largest Roman mosaic in Britain.

Dark-age remains

Largest Offa's Dyke, Welsh Borders [North, Mid and South Wales]; earthwork of ditches and banks stretching for 227 km [142 miles] from the River Wye to the North Wales coast, constructed by King Offa around AD784.

Towns and cities

Oldest city Ripon [Yorkshire and Humberside], city charter awarded to Ripon by Alfred the Great in AD886, first city charter in Britain.

Oldest town Colchester, Essex [East Anglia], site of Cunobelin's capital in AD10 and Roman town from AD45.

The Colchester Sphinx.

Oldest borough Barnstable, Devon [The West Country], chartered by King Athelstan in AD930.

First town chartered by Parliament Plymouth, Devon [The West Country], in 1439.

Largest city London, population 6 756 000.

Largest new town Milton Keynes [Thames and Chilterns], current population of 160 000 with a planned population by 2005 of 210 000.

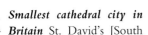

Smallest cathedral city in Britain St. David's [South Wales], with a population of 2000, the smallest cathedral city in the world.

Smallest cathedral city in England Wells, Somerset [West Country], with a population of less than 9000.

Smallest town Fordwich, Kent [South East England]; the population in 1991 was 252.

Top ten attractions charging admission

Madame Tussaud's [London]	2 547 000
Tower of London [London]	2 298 000
Alton Towers [Heart of England]	2 070 000
Natural History Museum [London]	1 534 000
Chessington Adventures [South East]	1 515 000
Blackpool Tower [North West]	1 426 000
Royal Academy [London]	1 309 000
Science Museum [London]	1 303 000
London Zoo [London]	1 250 000
Kew Gardens [London]	1 196 000

Most remote settlement Fair Isle [Scottish Highlands and Islands], 43 km [27 miles] from the next nearest inhabited island.

Oldest street Vicar's Close, Wells, Somerset [West Country], 14th-century, oldest inhabited street in Europe.

Medieval street The Shambles, York [Yorkshire and Humberside], best-preserved medieval street in Europe.

Longest name LlanfairPG, Anglesey [North Wales], full name: Llanfairpwllgwyngyllgogerychwyrndrobwllllantysiliogogogoch.

Largest group of listed buildings Albert Docks, Liverpool [North West England]; 3 ha [17½ acres] of docks surrounded by 120 000 m² [1 300 000 sq. ft] of Grade 1 listed warehouses dating from 1841–48.

Largest courtyard Great Court, Trinity College, Cambridge [East Anglia]. Built around a 1602 fountain the courtyard measures 104 m [340 ft] by 88 m [288 ft].

The South East

- LARGEST ROMAN PALACE – Fishbourne near Chichester in Sussex

- TALLEST ROMAN REMAIN – The Pharos in Dover Castle – 12 m [40 ft] still standing

- LARGEST CASTLE – Dover Castle – 13.74 ha [34 acres]

- OLDEST SCHOOL – Kings School in Canterbury – found in AD600

- LARGEST PRIVATE HOUSE – Knole House in Kent – 365 rooms

- OLDEST HOUSE – Eastry Court in Kent – AD603

Britain's largest castle – Dover.

HISTORIC BUILDINGS

Castles

Oldest original walls Richmond Castle [Yorkshire and Humberside], built 1080.

Oldest stone hall Scolland's Hall, Richmond Castle [Yorkshire and Humberside], built 1090.

First concentric Dover Castle, Dover [South East England], Norman structure of keep, inner curtain wall and outer curtain wall, replaced Saxon fortress and first Norman motte and bailey castle, construction completed by Henry II by 1189.

First purpose-built concentric Caerphilly Castle [South Wales]. The combined network of defensive moats and lakes covers 12 ha [30 acres] and encircles an outer curtain wall of 290 m [960 ft] diameter. Building started in 1268.

First designed for artillery Dartmouth Castle, Dartmouth [The West Country], built between 1481 and 1495 with gunports in the walls.

Longest continuously occupied Bamburgh [Northumbria], site occupied since AD550.

Largest Dover Castle, Dover [South East England], the outer curtain wall has 20 towers and encloses an area of 13.74 ha [34 acres].

Largest occupied Windsor Castle, Windsor [Thames and Chilterns], a figure-of-eight-shaped castle measuring 576 m [1890 ft] by 164 m [540 ft] and enclosing an area of 5.3 ha [13 acres].

Largest keep Colchester, Essex [East Anglia]; the keep is all that remains of the Norman castle and measures 46.3 m

Opposite: Caerphilly Castle, Britain's first purpose-built concentric castle.

London

As the nation's capital and largest city, London is, naturally, the home of many of Britain's national superlatives; the greatest and most spectacular of these are described in the sections of this guide devoted to historic, entertaining and commercial London.

Buckingham Palace.

[152 ft] by 33.5 m [110 ft] with walls 27.5 m [90 ft] high rising to 33.5 m [110 ft] at the corner towers, largest in Europe.

Thickest walls Flint Castle [North Wales], The Great Tower was built between 1277 and 1280 and has walls 7 m [23 ft] thick.

Last besieged Blair Castle, Blair Atholl [Scottish Highlands and Islands], unsuccessfully besieged by the Duke of Atholl in 1746.

Forts

Largest Fort George near Inverness [Scottish Highlands and Islands], built 1748–69; 640 m [2100 ft] long and an average of 189 m [620 ft] wide with a total area of 17.2 ha [42½ acres].

Towers

First stone Chepstow Castle, Chepstow [South Wales], built in AD1068 by William FitzOsbern.

Below: Dartmouth Castle.

Fortified bridges

Only surviving Monnow Bridge, Monmouth [South Wales]; 13th-century fortified gateway in middle of bridge, originally part of Monmouth town walls.

Guild halls

Oldest surviving Merchant Adventurers' Hall, York [Yorkshire and Humberside], founded in 1357.

Town walls

Best Elizabethan Berwick-upon-Tweed Ramparts [Northumbria], 1558-66, first town walls in Britain constructed with gun bastions and ramparts designed to survive artillery bombardment.

Best complete Chester Walls, Chester [North West England], 12th–14th-century, 3.2 km [2 miles] in circumference.

Gateways

Roman Newport Arch, Lincoln [East Midlands], the only complete Roman gateway in Britain.

Only preserved gate with barbican Walmgate Bar, York City Walls [Yorkshire and Humberside].

Christ Church Cathedral, Oxford.

Largest Chinese gateway Imperial Arch, Manchester [North West England], 9.2 m [30 ft] high, largest in Europe.

RELIGIOUS BUILDINGS

Origins

Oldest religious settlement Glastonbury, Somerset [West Country]; early Christian missionaries from Rome founded a settlement in AD166, although according to legend Joseph of Arimathea visited Glastonbury as early as AD63.

Cathedrals

Largest Liverpool Cathedral [North West England], 190 m [619 ft] long, 54 m [175 ft] wide at transept and 102 m [331 ft] tall.

Largest gothic York Minster, York [Yorkshire and Humberside]; 160 m [524 ft] long, 76 m [249 ft] wide across the transept, also the largest gothic cathedral in northern Europe.

Smallest Christ Church Cathedral, Oxford [Thames and Chilterns].

Longest Medieval Winchester Cathedral, Wiltshire [Southern England], built from 1079 onwards with extensive alterations in the 14th century, 169 m [556 ft] long, the longest in Europe.

Abbeys

Largest Fountain Abbey near Ripon [Yorkshire and Humberside], founded 1150.

Churches

Largest Collegiate Church of St. Peter, Westminster [Westminster Abbey] [London]; 161 m [530 ft] long and 31 m [102 ft] tall. Westminster Abbey also has the tallest nave in Britain.

Thames & Chilterns

- OLDEST WHITE HILL FIGURE – *Uffington White Horse in Oxfordshire – around 150BC*

- SMALLEST CATHEDRAL – *Christ Church Cathedral in Oxford*

- OLDEST MUSEUM – *Ashmolean Museum, Oxford – 1683*

- OLDEST LIBRARY – *Bodleian Library, Oxford – 1602*

- OLDEST UNIVERSITY – *Oxford University – 1167*

- OLDEST BOTANIC GARDENS – *Oxford University Botanic Gardens – 1621*

- OLDEST CONCERT HALL – *Holywell Music Room at Wadham College, Oxford – 1748*

- OLDEST PUBLIC HOUSE – *The Fighting Cocks, St. Albans – 11th-century on 8th-century foundations*

- LARGEST SAFARI PARK – *Woburn Safari Park, Woburn Abbey, Bedfordshire*

Oxford University Botanic Gardens.

Oldest in Britain Eileachan Naoimh [Scottish Highlands and Islands], St. Brendan's Cell built in AD542.

Oldest in England St. Martin's Church, Canterbury [South East England], founded by Bertha, wife of Ethelbert King of Kent pre AD597, used by St. Augustine to baptise Ethelbert.

Oldest Roman Catholic St. Etheldreda, Holborn [London], founded in 1251.

Oldest wooden St. Andrews, Greenstead, Essex [East Anglia], built around AD850.

Oldest round Church of the Holy Sepulchre, Cambridge [East Anglia], built in 1130.

Smallest Bremilham Church near Malmesbury, Wiltshire [West Country], 3.65 m [12 ft] square, only used once a year.

Smallest in regular use Culbone, Somerset [West Country], 10.66 m [35 ft] by 3.65 m [12 ft].

Chapels

Oldest non-conformist Horningsham, Wiltshire [West Country], founded in 1566.

Oldest methodist New Room, Broadmead, Bristol [West Country], 1739, the first Methodist chapel in the world.

Smallest St. Trillo's Chapel [North Wales], 3.65 m [12 ft] by 1.83 m [6 ft].

Synagogues

Largest Edgware Synagogue [London], built in 1959 with 1630 seats.

Towers

Only octagonal tower Ely Cathedral, Ely [East Anglia], built in 1335 the tower in turn supports a wooden lantern.

Only triangular tower All Saints Church, Maldon, Essex [East Anglia].

Top ten religious buildings

Westminster Abbey [London]	3 000 000
St. Paul's [London]	2 500 000
York Minster [Yorks and Humberside]	2 500 000
Canterbury Cathedral [South East]	2 250 000
Kings College Chapel [East Anglia]	1 000 000
Chester Cathedral [North West]	750 000
Norwich Cathedral [East Anglia]	589 000
Buckfast Abbey [West Country]	540 000
Salisbury Cathedral [West Country]	500 000
Durham Cathedral [Northumbria]	391 000

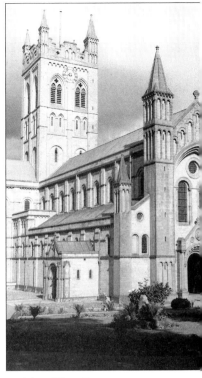

Spires

Tallest Salisbury Cathedral, Salisbury, Wiltshire [Southern England], cathedral constructed between 1220 and 1258, spire added in 1334, weighs 6400 tonnes and stands 122.7 m [404 ft] high.

Naves

Longest St. Albans Cathedral [Thames and Chilterns], uninterrupted length of 86.8 m [285 ft].

The dome of St. Paul's.

Tallest Westminster Abbey [London], 31 m [102 ft] high.

Domes

Only domed cathedral St. Paul's [London], the 33 m [107 ft] diameter dome is the only cathedral dome in Britain and the third largest in the world.

Crypts

Largest St. Paul's [London], the largest in Europe.

Buckfast Abbey, Devon.

Norman Canterbury Cathedral, Canterbury [South East England], completed by 1076, the largest in the world.

Saxon St. Wilfrid's Crypt at Hexham Abbey [Northumbria], built 674.

Gothic St. Mungo's Cathedral, Glasgow [Glasgow], the finest gothic crypt in Europe.

Vaulting

Longest gothic Exeter Cathedral, Exeter [The West Country], 90 m [300 ft] length covering both the nave and choir, built in 1275.

Bells

Oldest St. Botolph, Hardham, Sussex [South East England], 50 kg [1 cwt] bell dating from before AD1100.

Heaviest Great Paul, St. Paul's Cathedral [London], cast in 1881, 2.9 m [9 ft 6½ inches] in diameter and weighing 17 tons.

East Anglia

- ● **LOWEST LAND** – *Holme Fen in Cambridgeshire – 2.79 m [9 ft] below sea level*
- ● **OLDEST TOWN** – *Colchester, Essex – AD10*
- ● **LARGEST COURTYARD** – *Great Court, Trinity College, Cambridge – 104 m [340 ft] by 88 m [288 ft]*
- ● **LARGEST CASTLE KEEP** – *Colchester Castle – 46.3 m [152 ft] by 33.5 m [110 ft] with walls 27.5 m [90 ft] high*
- ● **OLDEST WOODEN CHURCH** – *St. Andrews at Greenstead in Essex – AD850*
- ● **SMALLEST PUBLIC HOUSE** – *The Nutshell in Bury St. Edmunds*
- ● **OLDEST WINDMILL** – *Bourn in Cambridgeshire – 1636*

Bourn Mill, Cambridgeshire.

Heaviest peal Liverpool Cathedral [North West England], 13 bells weighing 16½ tons, heaviest in the world.

Organs

Largest Liverpool Cathedral [North West England], 9704 pipes, the largest in Europe.

Oldest cover St. Stephen's Church, Old Radnor [Mid Wales], 15th-century linen organ case.

Stained glass

Oldest Section of a Jesse Window in York Minster, York [Yorkshire and Humberside], made around 1150.

Largest medieval Great East Window in York Minster, York [Yorkshire and Humberside], made in the 15th century.

Largest collection Liverpool Metropolitan Cathedral [North West England], 2000 tons of stained glass.

Largest individual window The East Window at Gloucester Cathedral [Heart of England], 21.94 m [72 ft] by 11.58 m [38 ft], created in 1350 to commemorate the Battle of Crècy.

Tapestry

Largest 'Christ in His Majesty' at Coventry Cathedral [Heart of England], 21.94 m [72 ft] tall and 11.88 m [39 ft] wide, designed by Graham Sutherland.

Crosses

Finest dark-age Ruthwell [Southern Scotland], 7th-century, 5.4 m [18 ft] long cross covered with Christian friezes and pagan runic symbols, regarded as the greatest dark-age religious relic in Europe.

Brasses

Oldest Stoke D'Abernon near Leatherhead [South East England], memorial to Sir John D'Abernon who died in 1277, the brass dates from around 1320.

CIVIC AND NATIONAL BUILDINGS

Palaces

Largest royal palace Buckingham Palace [London], the 600-room palace has a 186 m [610 ft] long east front and a ballroom 34 m [111 ft] long.

Halls

Largest medieval roof Westminster Hall [London], at a height of 27 m [90 ft] the 73 m [240 ft] by 21 m [69 ft] double hammerbeam roof is the largest medieval single span roof in the country.

Museums

Oldest Ashmolean Museum, Oxford [Thames and Chilterns], founded by Elias Ashmole in 1683.

Largest British Museum [London], founded in 1753 and opened to the public in 1759. The present building in Bloomsbury was built in 1823 – in 1990 the museum was visited by 4 769 000 people.

The Victoria & Albert Museum, London.

Largest railway museum National Railway Museum, York [Yorkshire and Humberside] – the largest in Europe.

Libraries

Oldest Bodleian Library, Oxford [Thames and Chilterns]. Founded by Sir Thomas Bodley in 1602, it now houses more than 4 000 000 books and manuscripts.

Oldest book-room Winchester Cathedral, Hampshire [Southern England]. The collection started in 1150, making it the oldest book-room in Europe.

Oldest subscription Leadhills [Southern Scotland] – Allan Ramsey's Miners Library was founded in 1741.

Largest British Library [London], is currently dispersed around 19 sites in London and a repository in Yorkshire. The total collection is 18 000 000 volumes. The new library building at St. Pancras will open in 1996 and will bring the collection under one roof.

Largest chained library Hereford Cathedral [Heart of England] – 1440 books and manuscripts from the 8th century onwards housed on 17th-century bookcases.

Opposite: The British Museum, London.

Top ten museums and art gallerys

British Museum [London]	4 769 000
National Gallery [London]	3 682 000
Tate Gallery [London]	1 562 000
Natural History Museum [London]	1 534 000
Royal Academy [London]	1 309 000
Science Museum [London]	1 303 000
Glasgow Art Gallery [Glasgow]	1 008 000
Victoria and Albert Museum [London]	962 000
Burrell Collection [Glasgow]	879 000
Jorvik Centre [Yorks and Humberside]	846 000

Above: St Andrew's University, Scotland.

Largest public reference Mitchell Library, Glasgow [Glasgow]. Founded in 1874, it contains 1 000 000 volumes, the largest public reference library in Europe.

First Carnegie Library Dunfermline [Scottish Highlands and Islands], birthplace of Andrew Carnegie in 1835 and the site of the first of the 300 Carnegie Libraries that he sponsored around the world, founded in 1881.

Universities

Largest London University [London] – 79 377 students registered in 1988/89.

Oldest in Britain Oxford University, Oxford [Thames and Chilterns], founded in 1167.

Oldest in Scotland St. Andrew's [Scottish Highlands and Islands], founded in 1411.

Largest non-campus The Open University, Milton Keynes [Thames and Chilterns], founded in 1969 as a distance learning university, 104 799 students, post-graduate students and short course students registered in 1990.

Schools

Oldest King's School, Canterbury [South East England], established by St. Augustine around AD600.

Oldest public Winchester College, Winchester, Hampshire [Southern England], founded in 1382.

Largest Exmouth Community College, Devon [The South West], 2036 pupils in 1990/91.

Hospitals

Oldest St Peter's, York [Yorkshire and Humberside], founded around AD937, now absorbed into St. Leonard's Hospital.

Oldest on same site St. Bartholomew's Hospital [London], the second hospital in Britain, founded in 1123 and still on the same site.

Largest Hartwood Hospital, Shotts [Southern Scotland], 1600 beds for mentally-ill patients.

Largest general St. James University Hospital, Leeds [Yorkshire and Humberside], 1432 beds.

Prisons

Largest Wandsworth Prison [London], official capacity 1266 prisoners.

Cemeteries

Largest Brookwood Cemetery, Surrey [South East England], covers 200 ha [500 acres] and holds 225 000 internments.

Crematoria

Oldest Woking, Surrey [South East England], first used on 26 March 1885.

Town halls

Oldest still in use Exeter Guildhall, Exeter [The South West], built in 1468 and still in continuous use by Exeter City Council.

Heart of England

- *LARGEST BIRD RESERVE – Slimbridge, Gloucestershire – 3300 birds*
- *LARGEST ROMAN MOSAIC – Woodchester, Gloucestershire – 14.3 m² [45 sq. ft]*
- *LARGEST STAINED GLASS WINDOW – East Window, Gloucester Cathedral – 21.94 m [72 ft] by 11.58 m [38 ft]*
- *LARGEST TAPESTRY – Christ in His Majesty at Coventry Cathedral – 21.94 m [72 ft] by 11.88 m [38 ft]*
- *OLDEST MUSIC FESTIVAL – Three Choirs Festival – founded in 1724*
- *LARGEST THEME PARK – Alton Towers – 125 rides and attractions*
- *LARGEST VAT – Strongbow Vat at Bulmers in Hereford – 74 099 hl [1 630 000 gallons] capacity*

Alton Towers.

Embassies

Largest United States Embassy, Grosvenor Square [London], opened in 1960 with 600 rooms on seven floors providing 236 895 m² [2 550 000 sq. feet] of useable space.

Clocks

Oldest Salisbury Cathedral, Salisbury [West Country], faceless clock dating from 1386.

The Royal Liver Building, Liverpool.

Largest Royal Liver Building, Liverpool [North West England]. The dial's diameter is 7.7 m [25 ft], the minute hand is 4.3 m [14 ft] long and 1 m [3 ft] wide.

North West England

- **LARGEST ROMAN AMPHITHEATRE** – *Chester*

- **LARGEST GROUP OF LISTED BUILDINGS** – *Albert Docks – 1200 m² [130 000 sq. ft] of grade 1 Victorian warehouses*

- **LARGEST CATHEDRAL** – *Liverpool Cathedral*

- **LARGEST CLOCK** – *Royal Liver Building in Liverpool – 7.7 m [25 ft] in diameter*

- **LONGEST STONE BRIDGE** – *Grosvenor Bridge at Chester – 61 m [200 ft] long*

- **LONGEST ROAD TUNNEL** – *Queensway Tunnel, Liverpool – 4.6 km [2.87 miles]*

Albert Docks, Liverpool.

Above: Warwick Castle.

Stately homes

Most visited Warwick Castle [Heart of England], 14th-century castle and house, visited by 685 000 people in 1990.

Tallest fountain Emperor Fountain, Chatsworth House, Peak District [East Midlands], 79 m [260 ft] high, created by Joseph Paxton in 1834.

Dome

Largest in Britain Bell Sports Centre, Perth [Scottish Highlands and Islands], measuring 67 m [222 ft] in diameter.

Largest in England Royal Devonshire Hospital, Buxton, Peak District [East Midlands], measuring 50 m [164 ft] in diameter, constructed in 1881.

ENTERTAINMENT

Art

Largest painting 'Triumph of Peace', the ceiling of the Painted Hall in the Royal Naval College, Greenwich [London]. Painted by Sir James Thornhill between 1707 and 1727, it measures 32.3 m [106 ft] by 15.4 m [51 ft].

Largest mural Royal Liverpool Children's Hospital, Liverpool [North West], 497.7 m [1633 ft] long, covering a total area of 1668.7 m² [17 963 sq. ft].

Largest tapestry 'Christ in His Majesty' at Coventry Cathedral [Heart of England], 21.94 m [72 ft] tall and 11.88 m [39 ft] wide, designed by Graham Sutherland.

Concert halls

Oldest Holywell Music Room, Wadham College, Oxford [Thames and Chilterns]. First used in 1748, it is the oldest still in use.

Cinemas

Largest The Odeon, Leicester Square [London], with 1983 seats.

Biggest screen IMAX, Bradford [Yorkshire and Humberside], measuring 19 m [62 ft] by 16.5 m [54 ft].

Largest sound stage Pinewood Studios [Thames and Chilterns], 102 m by 42 m by 12 m [336 × 139 × 41 ft], built in 1976 for the James Bond film, *The Spy Who Love Me*. It is the largest in the world.

Theatres

Oldest still in use Theatre Royal, Bristol [West Country]. The foundation stone was laid on 30 November 1764 and the theatre opened to the public on 30 May 1766.

Festivals

Largest arts festivals Edinburgh Festival [Edinburgh]. Founded in 1947, it is the largest in the world.

Oldest music festival Three Choirs, Gloucester, Hereford and Worcester Cathedrals [Heart of England]. The annual festival rotates between the three sites. It was first held in 1724.

FOOD AND DRINK

Hotels

Largest Grosvenor House Hotel, Park Lane [London]. Opened in 1929, it has 470 rooms in an eight-storey building covering 1 ha [2½ acres].

Tallest London Forum Hotel, Cromwell Road [London], 27 storeys, 132.24 m [380 ft] high.

Most beds London Forum Hotel, Cromwell Road [London], opened in 1973 with 1859 beds.

Most remote Garvault Hotel, Kinbrace [Scottish Highlands and Islands], 25.7 km [16 miles] from its nearest competitor.

Public houses

Oldest The Fighting Cocks, St. Albans [Thames and Chilterns]. It is an 11th-

Opposite: the diminutive Nutshell, Bury St. Edmunds.

The Theatre Royal, Bristol.

century structure on 8th-century foundations.

Highest Tan Hill, Arkengarthdale, Yorkshire Dales [Yorkshire and Humberside], is 528 m [1723 ft] above sea level.

Largest Downham Tavern, Bromley, Kent [South East England]. Built in 1930, it has two large bars with 13.7 m [45 ft] of counter space and can cater for 1000 customers.

Smallest The Nutshell, Bury St. Edmunds [East Anglia], where the ground floor measures 4.82 m [15 ft 10 in] by 2.28 m [7 ft 6 in].

Smallest bar The Front Bar, The Dove, Hammersmith riverside [London], measures 127 cm [4 ft 2 in] by 239 cm [7 ft 10 in].

Longest counter The Long Bar, The Cornwall Coliseum Auditorium, Carlyon Bay, Cornwall [The South West], measures 31.8 m [104 ft 3 in] long and has 34 beer and lager dispensers.

Restaurants

Largest fast food Talbot Restaurant, Alton Towers [Heart of England], which serves 2000 meals per hour.

Butlins Holiday Camp, Skegness.

petition for married couples who can prove they have been happily married for a year and a day. The prize being a side of pig, it was first held in 1244.

Holiday camps

First Butlins Holiday Camp at Skegness, Lincolnshire [East Midlands], which opened in 1937.

Seaside piers

Longest Southend on Sea, Essex [East Anglia], measuring 2158 m [7080 ft] long, built in 1890 and extended in 1930, the longest in the world.

Below: Southend Pier.

Largest fish and chip Harry Ramsden's Fish and Chip Emporium, Guiseley [Yorkshire and Humberside], founded in 1928. The 140 staff serve more than 1 000 000 customers a year using 213 tons of fish and 356 tons of potatoes.

Highest The Ptarmigan Observation Restaurant near Aviemore [Scottish Highlands and Islands], stands 1112 m [3650 ft] above sea level.

Most visited Alton Towers [Heart of England] – 2 070 000 paying visitors in 1990.

Largest indoor Metroland, Gateshead MetroCentre [Northumbria], which is largest in Europe.

Largest television-based Granada Studio Tours, Manchester [North West England], which opened in 1988.

Competitions

Oldest Dunmow Flitch, Great Dunmow, Essex [East Anglia], a com-

LEISURE

Fun fairs

Most visited Blackpool Pleasure Beach, Blackpool [North West England] – 6 500 000 visitors per year; Britain's most popular free attraction.

Theme parks

Largest Alton Towers [Hearts of England], 125 rides and attractions in 81 ha [200 acres].

Top ten attractions with free admission

Blackpool Pleasure Beach [North West]	6 500 000
Liverpool Albert Docks [North West]	6 000 000
British Museum [London]	4 769 000
Strathclyde Park [Southern Scotland]	4 200 000
National Gallery [London]	3 682 000
Brighton Palace Pier [South East]	3 500 000
Westminster Abbey [London]	3 000 000
Yarmouth Pleasure Beach [East Anglia]	2 600 000
St. Paul's Cathedral [London]	2 500 000
York Minster [Yorks and Humberside]	2 500 000

Most visited The Palace Pier, Brighton [South East England]. Built in 1899, it attracted 3 500 000 visitors in 1990.

Only town with three piers Blackpool [North West England].

Marina

Largest Brighton Marina, Brighton [South East England], opened in 1978 with berths for 2000 boats – the largest man-made marina in Europe.

Model villages

Oldest Beckonscot, Beaconsfield [Thames and Chilterns]. Founded in 1929, it is the oldest in the world.

Steam railways

Oldest Talyllyn Railway, Towyn [North Wales], which runs for 11 km [7 miles] from Towyn to Abergynolwyn, opened in 1865 and has been in continuous use ever since. It became the first preserved steam railway in Britain when 'rescued' in 1951.

Oldest coaches Talyllyn Railway, Towyn [North Wales]. Built in 1865, they are the oldest passenger coaches in the world still in regular use.

Camera obscura

Largest Aberystwyth [Mid Wales], displays 96 km [60 miles] of Mid and

Below: the Marina, Brighton.

East Midlands

- **LARGEST CAVE MOUTH** – Peak Cavern, Castleton – 10 m [33 ft] high by 30 m [100 ft] wide

- **FIRST NATIONAL PARK** – Peak District – 17th April 1951

- **BEST-PRESERVED ROMAN GATEWAY** – Newport Arch, Lincoln

- **TALLEST FOUNTAINS** – Emperor Fountain at Chatsworth House – can rise to 79 m [260 ft]

- **TALLEST TV MAST** – Horncastle, Lincolnshire – 387.12 m [1272 ft]

The Emperor Fountain – Britain's tallest.

North Wales landscape. It is the largest in the world.

Wax works

Most visited Madame Tussauds [London], founded in 1833 and visited by more than 2 500 000 people per year.

Horse fair

Largest Appleby-in-Westmorland [Cumbria], held every June since 1685.

Cable cars

Longest Llandudno Chairlift, Llandudno [North Wales] – 1622 m [5320 ft] ride to the top of Great Orme.

NATURE

Botanic gardens

Oldest Oxford University Botanic Gardens, Oxford [Thames and Chilterns], founded in 1621 by Henry Danvers, Earl of Danby, as the University's Physic Garden.

Oldest rhododendron collection Edinburgh Royal Botanic Gardens [Edinburgh]. The rhododendron collection was started in 1823 and is the largest collection in Britain.

Oldest pot plant Encephalartos altensteinii in the Royal Botanic Gardens at Kew [London], a single cycad taken to Kew from South Africa in 1775.

Rarest plant Encephalartos woodii in the Royal Botanic Gardens at Kew [London], the only known specimen in the world of a plant the origins of which go back more than 200 million years.

Tallest flagstaff The Royal Botanic Gardens at Kew [London]. The 68 m

Opposite: the interior of the Temperate House at the Royal Botanical Gardens, Kew.

[225 ft] tall flagstaff was erected on 7th May 1958.

Tallest pagoda The Royal Botanic Gardens at Kew [London] – 50 m [163 ft] tall, built in 1761.

Arboretum

Widest range Westonbirt Arboretum, Tetbury [Heart of England], has 14000 trees and shrubs in 200 ha [500 acres] of woodland and 40 ha [100 acres] of downland, founded in 1829.

Parks

Largest privately owned Woburn Abbey Park, Woburn Sands [Thames and Chilterns], the Duke of Bedford's estate covering 1200 ha [3000 acres].

Gardens

Earliest English Claremont Landscape Garden, Surrey [South East England], created by Bridgeman and Vanbrugh between 1711 and 1726 and extended, in the same style, from 1727 onwards by

Powis Castle Gardens.

Hampton Court, home of the Great Vine.

William Kent and Capability Brown. It is the earliest 'natural English' landscape garden in Britain.

Earliest formal Powis Castle Gardens, Welshpool [Mid Wales], which has four hanging terraces each 180 m [600 ft] long with lead statues dotted amongst the foliage. It was laid out between 1688 and 1720.

Largest vine The Great Vine at Hampton Court [London]. Planted in 1768, it has a girth of 215.9 cm [85 in], branches 34.7 m [114 ft] long and yields 318.8 kg [703 lbs] of black grapes each year.

Oldest hedge maze Hampton Court [London], created by George London and Henry Wise in 1690.

Largest hedge maze Longleat House, Warminster, Wiltshire [West Country]. Opened on 6 June 1978, it covers an area of 67.66 m [381 ft] by 57 m [187 ft] and contains 2.72 km [1.69 miles] of paths flanked by 16 180 yew trees.

Zoos

First The Zoological Society of London, Regent's Park, founded in 1826 by Sir Humphrey Davy and Sir Stamford Raffles. The site was laid out by Decimus Burton in 1827 and opened to the public on 27 April 1828, making it the first public zoo in the world.

Safari parks

Largest Woburn Safari Park, Woburn Abbey, Bedfordshire [Thames and Chilterns].

Farms

Earliest Hembury, Devon [The South West]. This Neolithic farm has remains dated at around 4000BC.

Largest The hill farms of the Scottish Grampians.

Largest cultivated Elvedon, Suffolk [East Anglia]. The total farm area is 9000 ha [22 500 acres] of which 4500 ha [11 000 acres] are under active cultivation.

Largest turkey Bernard Matthews plc, Great Witchingham, Norfolk [East Anglia]. With 9 000 000 turkeys, it is the largest in the world.

Inmates of Woburn Safari Park, Bedfordshire.

PRIVATE HOUSING

Houses

Largest Knole House, Kent [South East England]; started in 1456 and extended in 1603, the house has 365 rooms and 52 staircases.

Largest Tudor Burghley House, Stamford [East Midlands], built between 1553 and 1587.

Oldest Eastry Court near Sandwich, Kent [South East England], with some timber and infilling dating from AD603.

Smallest The Quay, Conwy [North Wales], a 19th-century fisherman's cottage. There are two small rooms and a staircase – the external dimensions are 182 cm [72 in] frontage, 254 cm [100 in] depth and 309 cm [122 in] in height.

First round house Belle Island, Bowness-on-Windermere [Cumbria], built in 1774.

Council estates

Largest Becontree estate, Barking [London]. This 672 ha [1670 acres] estate was built in 1929 and has 26 822 houses and an estimated population of 90 000.

Superlative SUPERLATIVES
TOPS IN EUROPE

In addition to our world beaters there are many other British superlatives that are the best in Europe:

THE LARGEST MAN-MADE LAKES – Kielder Water, Northumberland [by volume] and Rutland Water, Leicestershire [by area]

Rocket *replica, National Railway Museum.*

THE LARGEST MAN-MADE FOREST – Kielder Forest, Northumberland

THE LARGEST ARTIFICIAL MOUND – Silbury Hill, Wiltshire

THE LARGEST HILL FORT – Maiden Castle, Dorset

THE OLDEST INHABITED STREET – Vicar's Close, Wells, Somerset

THE LARGEST CHINESE GATEWAY – Imperial Arch, Manchester

THE LARGEST CRYPT – St. Paul's, London

Above: Vicar's Close, Wells.

Above: Kielder Forest, Northumberland.

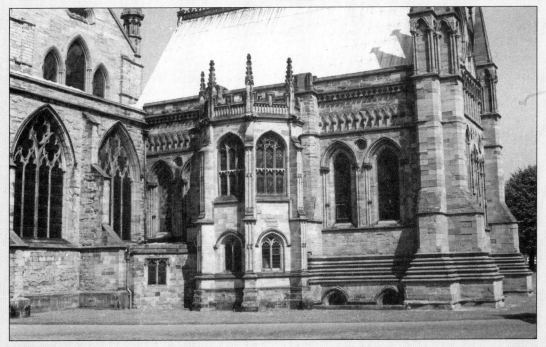

Hereford Cathedral, home of Europe's largest chained library.

THE LARGEST ORGAN – *Liverpool Cathedral*

THE OLDEST BOOK-ROOM – *Winchester Cathedral*

Harland and Wolff Shipyard, Belfast.

THE LARGEST CHAINED LIBRARY – *Hereford Cathedral*

THE LARGEST PUBLIC REFERENCE LIBRARY – *The Mitchell Library, Glasgow*

THE LARGEST INDOOR THEME PARK – *Gateshead Metroland*

THE LARGEST TV THEME PARK – *Granada Studio Tours, Manchester*

THE LARGEST MAN-MADE MARINA – *Brighton, Sussex*

THE LARGEST RAILWAY MUSEUM – *The National Railway Museum, York*

THE LONGEST RAIL TUNNEL – *Eurotunnel, Folkestone, Kent*

THE LONGEST CANTILEVER BRIDGE – *The Forth Rail Bridge*

THE LONGEST CABLE-STAYED BRIDGE – *Queen Elizabeth Bridge, Dartford–Tilbury*

THE DEEPEST ROAD CUTTING – *M62 at Dean Head*

THE LARGEST CRANES – *Goliath and Sampson, Harland and Wolff Shipyard, Belfast*

THE LARGEST SHOPPING CENTRE – *Gateshead MetroCentre*

Flat blocks

Tallest Shakespeare Tower, Barbican [London], was built in 1971 with 44 storeys containing 116 flats, 127.77 m [419 ft 2½ in] tall.

Largest The Barbican [London], 16 ha [40 acres] site containing 2011 flats.

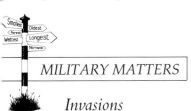

MILITARY MATTERS

Invasions

Last successful Led by William Duke of Normandy, William the Conqueror, Hastings [South East England], 4 October 1066.

Last Carregwastad Point, Fishguard [South Wales], 22 February 1797, when Irish American General William Tate landed with a force of 1200 French soldiers. They surrendered to local troops and villagers two days later.

Battlefields

Norman Conquest Battle of Hastings, Senlac Hill near Hastings [South East England], 14 October 1066, when William the Conqueror defeated the Saxon army of King Harold and started the total Norman conquest of England.

Last battle in Britain Culloden near Inverness [Scottish Highlands and Islands], 16 April 1746, when Bonnie Prince Charlie lost to George II's son, the Duke of Cumberland.

Last battle in England Sedgemoor, Somerset [West Country], 6 July 1685, James Duke of Monmouth was defeated by English crown troops.

Army barracks

Oldest purpose-built Berwick-upon-Tweed [Northumbria], built by Vanbrugh in 1719.

Opposite: Sedgemoor, Somerset, site of the last battle on English soil.

Yorkshire and Humberside

- *LARGEST CAVE SYSTEM – Ease Gill on Whernside – 66 km [41 miles] of explored caverns and passages*

- *OLDEST CITY – Ripon – city charter granted by Alfred the Great in AD886*

- *OLDEST ORIGINAL CASTLE WALLS – Richmond Castle – AD1080*

- *OLDEST SURVIVING STONE HALL – Scolland's Hall in Richmond Castle – AD1090*

- *OLDEST SURVIVING GUILD HALL – Merchant Adventurers' Hall in York – 1357*

- *OLDEST STAINED GLASS – in York Minister – 1150*

- *TALLEST CHIMNEY – Drax Power Station – 259 m [850 ft] tall*

- *TALLEST TOWER – Emley Moor TV Tower – 329.18 m [1080 ft] tall*

The town hall, Ripon.

The entrance to Portsmouth Harbour.

Longest continuous service HMS *Victory*, Portsmouth [Southern England], built in 1765 and still, 227 years later, a commissioned ship-of-the-line. Sea-going for more than 150 years and in dry dock since 1921, it was Admiral Nelson's flagship at the Battle of Trafalgar and is the oldest commissioned ship in the world.

Above: HMS Victory.

Oldest warship afloat HMS *Unicorn*, Dundee [Scottish Highlands and Islands], a 46-gun, 46 m [152 ft] long frigate launched in 1824.

First iron-hulled warship HMS *Warrior*, Portsmouth [Southern England], launched in 1860, the first iron-hulled, armoured warship in the world.

Naval establishments

First dry dock Portsmouth [Southern England], constructed on the orders of Henry VII in the early 16th century.

Ships

Oldest Warship The *Mary Rose*, Portsmouth [Southern England]. Henry VIII's flagship, weighing 700 tons and carrying 91 cannons, sank in 1545 and was lifted by salvage teams in 1982.

Top six historic ships

Cutty Sark, *Greenwich [London]*	*411 000*
HMS Victory, *Portsmouth [Southern England]*	*340 000*
Mary Rose, *Portsmouth [Southern England]*	*333 000*
HMS Belfast *[London]*	*230 000*
HMS Warrior, *Portsmouth [Southern England]*	*175 000*
SS Great Britain, *Bristol [West Country]*	*145 000*

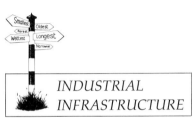

INDUSTRIAL INFRASTRUCTURE

Railways

First commercial passenger line Liverpool to Manchester Railway [North West England], built by George Stephenson and opened in 1830 – the first in the world.

First commercial freight line Stockton to Darlington Railway [Northumbria], built by George Stephenson and opened on 27 September 1825 – first in the world.

First passenger station Liverpool Road Station, Manchester [North West England]. Opened in 1830, it was first in the world.

Largest passenger station Clapham Junction [London], an 11.22 ha [27¾ acres] site with 16 platforms with a total length of 3243 m [10 682 ft].

Station with largest number of platforms Waterloo [London], which has 19 mainline platforms.

Station with longest platforms Gloucester [Heart of England], where they measure 602.69 m [1977 ft 4 in].

Busiest station Clapham Junction [London], with 2200 trains per day.

Highest station Corrour [Scottish Highlands and Islands], which stands 410.5 m [1347 ft] above sea level.

Clapham Junction – an aerial view.

First railway bridge Causey Arch, Tanfield Waggonway [Northumbria]. It was built in 1725 and has a span of 32 m [105 ft].

Longest rail bridge Tay Railway Bridge, Dundee [Scottish Highlands and Islands], which opened on 20 June 1887. It has a multiple arch bridge with 85 arches – total length 3552 m [11 653 ft] – the longest in Europe.

Longest rail tunnel The Eurotunnel, Folkestone [South East England], linking Britain and France with two rail tunnels and a service tunnel. Tunnel breakthrough occurred on 30 October 1990. The length between tunnel portals is 49.94 km [31.03 miles] of which 37 km [23 miles] are under the English Channel. It is the second longest rail tunnel in the world.

First railway embankment Tanfield Waggonway [Northumbria], built in 1725.

Oldest electric railway Volk's Electric Railway, Brighton [South East England], which was opened in 1883.

Rack and pinion railway Snowdonia Mountain Railway [North Wales], is Britain's only working rack and pinion railway and runs from Llanberis to the summit of Snowdon. It is 8 km [5 miles] long and climbs 900 m [2950 ft].

Underground railways

First London Underground or Tube [London]. The first section from Paddington to Farringdon Street was opened on 10 January 1863, making it the oldest in the world.

Longest tunnel Morden to East Finchley on the Northern Line, London Underground [London]. At 27.84 km [17½ miles], it is the third longest tunnel in the world.

Roads

Oldest known Sweet Way, Somerset [West Country]. The trackway was built

The Snowdonia Mountain Railway.

from felled trees, and dating has shown that the trees were felled during 3807–3806BC.

Longest A1 London to Edinburgh – 650 km [404 miles].

Highest public road A93 at Cairnwell [Scottish Highlands and Islands], which is 670 m [2199 ft] above sea level.

Widest road M61 Linnyshaw Moss, Worsley [North West], which has 17 carriageways.

Steepest road Chimney Bank, Rosedale Abbey [Yorkshire and Humberside], signposted as '1 in 3'.

Longest ring road M25 London Orbital Motorway, which is 195.5 km [121½ miles]. It opened in October 1986.

Longest viaduct M6 Gravelly Hill to Castle Bromwich [Heart of England], which is 4.8 km [2.97 miles].

Longest ford Violet's Lane, Furneux Pelham, Hertfordshire [Thames and Chilterns] – 903 m [2961 ft].

Violet's Lane, Hertfordshire.

First stretch of motorway M6 Preston [North West]. The 13.6 km [8.5 miles] Preston bypass was opened on 5 December 1958 by Harold Macmillan. It now forms part of the M6 but was the first stretch of motorway in the country, predating the M1 by one year.

Highest motorway M62 at Windy Hill [Yorkshire and Humberside], standing 371 m [1220 ft] above sea level.

First motorway service area M1 at Watford Gap [Thames and Chilterns], which opened on 2 November 1959.

Deepest cutting M62 at Dean Head [Yorkshire and Humberside]; 55.7 m [183 ft] deep, the deepest cutting in Europe.

Oldest milestone Stanegate near Chesterholme [Northumbria]; Roman stone dating from AD150.

Longest road bridge Humber Road Bridge near Hull [Yorkshire and Humberside], with a total length of 2220 m [7283 ft], and length between towers of 1410 m [4626 ft]. It opened on 17 July 1981 and is the longest suspension bridge in the world.

Car parks

Largest National Exhibition Centre, Birmingham [Heart of England], which provides spaces for 15 000 cars and 200 coaches.

Petrol stations

Largest M4 Leigh Delamere Service Area, Wiltshire [Southern England],

Birmingham's NEC has Britain's largest car park.

Northumbria

- **LARGEST ROMAN REMAIN** – *Hadrian's Wall* – *122 km [76 miles]*
- **BEST-PRESERVED ROMAN FORT** – *Housesteads on Hadrian's Wall*
- **OLDEST MILESTONE** – *Stanegate near Chesterholme* – *AD150*
- **OLDEST BARRACKS** – *Berwick-on-Tweed* – *1719*

The best-preserved Roman fort – Housesteads, Northumberland.

which opened on 3 January 1972, covers 17.4 ha [43 acres] and has 48 petrol and diesel dispensers.

Canals

Earliest Fossdyke, Lincoln [East Midlands]. Constructed by the Romans around AD100, it is 17.7 km [11 miles] long.

First modern Duke of Bridgewater's, Worsley [North West England], constructed by James Brindley and opened in 1761.

Highest Macclesfield Canal [East Midlands], 157.5 m [519 ft] above sea level.

Longest ship canal Manchester Ship Canal [North West England], 64 km [39.7 miles], built between 1887–94, the eighth longest in the world.

Oldest ship canal Exeter Canal [The South West], opened in 1566.

Oldest lock gates Exeter Canal [The South West], 1566.

Largest lock Portbury, Bristol [West Country]. It opened in August 1977, and is 366 m [1200 ft] long, 42.7 m [140 ft] wide and 20.2 m [66 ft] deep.

Longest flight of locks Worcester and Birmingham Canal, Terdebigge [Heart of England], where 36 locks drop the canal by 78.9 m [259 ft] over a distance of 4 km 2.5 miles].

Longest aqueduct Pont Cysylltau [North Wales], designed by Thomas Telford and opened in 1805. Nineteen arches carry the canal over a length of 307 m [1007 ft].

Airports

Busiest Heathrow Airport [London], which handled 344 841 flights and 39 610 550 passengers in 1990. Of these, 31 525 476 were international passengers, making Heathrow the busiest international airport in the world.

Seaports

Busiest passenger Dover [South East England], where the Outer Harbour covers 344 ha [1.33 sq. miles], and the port handles over 12 000 000 passengers per year.

Ships

Oldest surviving Holme-on-Spalding Moor near Hull [Yorkshire and Humberside]. Re-discovered in 1984, 13.71 m [45 ft] long, it was constructed around 300BC.

First iron-hulled SS *Great Britain*, Bristol [West Country] – 98 m [322 ft] long, built by Isambard Kingdom Brunel in 1843. It was the world's first iron-hulled, screw-driven passenger ship.

Bridges

Oldest Tarr Steps, Exmoor [West Country]. It is a clapper bridge of uncertain age but is certainly pre-Roman.

First iron Ironbridge, Telford [Heart of England], which was constructed by Abraham Darby III in 1779, making it the first in the world.

Ironbridge, Telford.

Dover, Britain's busiest seaport.

First tubular Britannia Tubular Bridge, Menai Strait [North Wales], built by Robert Stephenson in 1850.

First suspension Wynch Suspension Bridge, River Tees [Northumbria], built in 1741.

First large suspension Menai Strait Bridge [North Wales], built by Thomas Telford in 1826; 386 m [1265 ft] long.

Longest suspension Humber Road Bridge near Hull [Yorkshire and Humberside], which has a total length 2220

m [7283 ft], and length between towers 1410 m [4626 ft]. It opened on 17 July 1981 – the longest suspension bridge in the world.

Longest suspension bridge in Scotland Forth Road Bridge – opened in 1964, total length 1006 m [5979 ft], the eighth longest in the world.

Longest suspension bridge in Wales Severn Bridge [South Wales], which opened in 1966. Its total length is 988 m [3241 ft] making it the ninth longest in the world.

Longest stone Grosvenor Bridge, Chester [North West], designed by Thomas

Opposite: the Menai Strait Suspension Bridge.

Harrison in 1802 and opened in 1832 – 61 m [200 ft] span.

Longest cantilever Forth Railway Bridge [Southern Scotland]. Completed in January 1890, it carries a double railway line over the Forth and is 521 m [1710 ft] long – the second longest in the world.

Longest cable-stayed Queen Elizabeth Bridge, Tilbury to Dartford [London and South East England]. Opened in August 1991 and 2872 m [8702 ft] long, it is the longest in Europe.

Longest steel arched Runcorn–Widnes Bridge [North West], which was opened on 21 July 1961 with a central span of 329.8 m [1082 ft].

Above: the Humber Bridge, Humberside.

Longest illuminated Forth Railway Bridge [Southern Scotland], floodlit with 1000 high-powered sodium flood-lights using 40 km [25 miles] of cabling. The lights were first turned on in 1990 to celebrate the centenary of the Bridge's construction and will remain illuminated until the year 2000. It is the largest illuminated bridge in the world.

Longest cycle bridge Cambridge Railway Station, Cambridge [East Anglia], where the cycleway bridges 17 railway tracks. Supported by a 35 m [114.82 ft] tower, it is 237.6 m [779.52 ft] long.

Cumbria

- *LARGEST NATIONAL PARK – The Lake District – 2292 km² [885 sq. miles]*
- *THE FIRST ROUND HOUSE – Belle Island, Windermere*
- *THE LARGEST HORSE-FAIR – Appleby-in-Westmorland – first held in 1685*
- *THE OLDEST WORKING STEAM YACHT – Gondola, Coniston Water*

The Gondola, *Coniston Water.*

First railway bridge Causey Arch, Tanfield Waggonway [Northumbria] – 32 m [105 ft] span built in 1725.

Longest railway bridge Tay Railway Bridge, Dundee [Scottish Highlands and Islands]. It opened on 20 June 1887 and is a multiple arch bridge with 85 arches; total length is 3552 m [11 653 ft], making it the longest in Europe.

Tunnels

Longest rail The Eurotunnel, Folkestone [South East England], linking Britain and France with two rail tunnels and a service tunnel; tunnel breakthrough happened on 30 October 1990. The length between tunnel portals is 49.94 km [31.03 miles] of which 37 km [23 miles] are under the English Channel. It is the second longest rail tunnel in the world.

Longest underground railway Morden to East Finchley, Northern Line, London Underground [London], 27.84 km [17½ miles], the third longest in the world.

Longest road Queensway Tunnel, Liverpool [North West England], 4.6 km [2.87 miles] long, opened in 1934.

Longest canal Stanedge Tunnel [Yorkshire and Humberside], built between 1794 and 1811, 5.21 km [3 miles 1254 ft] long.

Longest water supply London Ring Main [London], currently under construction and due to be completed by 1994, total length 76 km [47.2 miles].

Flood barriers

Largest Thames Barrier, Woolwich [London], opened in May 1984; total length when gates are raised is 555 m [1830 ft], height 20 m [66 ft]. Six large and two small gates rotate from the riverbed, large gates are each 61 m [200 ft] wide and weigh 1300 tons. It is the largest movable barrier in the world.

Dams

Most massive Kielder Dam [Northumbria] – 1140 m [3740 ft] long and 52 m [170 ft] high.

Tallest Llyn Brianne [Mid Wales]. Completed in November 1971, it stands 91 m [298½ ft] high.

Longest Hanningfield Dam, Essex [East Anglia], measuring 2088 m [6850 ft] long.

Reservoirs

Largest volume Kielder Water [Northumbria], contains 2 000 000 000 hl [44 000 000 000 gallons] in a lake with a perimeter of 43.4 km [27 miles] and a surface area of 10.85 km² [4.19 sq. miles] – the largest in Europe.

Largest area Rutland Water [East Midlands], with a total surface area of 12.54

Scotland

- OLDEST ROCK FORMATIONS – North West Highlands – 2 800 000 000 years old

- HIGHEST MOUNTAIN – Ben Nevis, Fort William – 1343 m [4406 ft]

- LONGEST LAKE – Loch Ness – 38.99 km [24.23 miles]

- DEEPEST LAKE – Loch Morar – 310 m [1017 ft]

- TALLEST CLIFF – Conachair, St. Kilda – 396 m [1300 ft]

- LONGEST WATERFALL – Eas a Chual Alainn, Sutherland – 200 m [568 ft]

- OLDEST MAN-MADE STRUCTURE – stone rings on Jura – dating from 6000BC

- MOST REMOTE HUMAN SETTLEMENT – Fair Island – 43 km [27 miles] from its nearest neighbour

- LAST CASTLE TO BE BESIEGED – Blair Castle, Blair Atholl – 1746

- LARGEST FORT – Fort George near Inverness – 17.2 ha [42½ acres] in area

- OLDEST CHURCH – Eileachan Naoimh – built around AD543

- LARGEST DOME – Bell Sports Centre, Perth – 67 m [222 ft] in diameter

- HIGHEST RESTAURANT – The Ptarmigan Observation Restaurant near Aviemore – 1160 m [3650 ft] above sea level

- LAST BATTLE – Culloden near Inverness – 16th April, 1746

- LONGEST RAILWAY BRIDGE – Tay Bridge, Dundee – 3552 m [11653 ft]

Brooding Ben Nevis.

km² [4.84 sq. miles], the largest in Europe.

Largest totally artificial Queen Mary Reservoir [London]. Opened in 1925, its 6.32 km [3.93 mile] perimeter retains a surface area of 286 ha [707 acres].

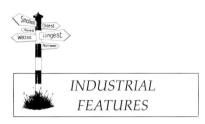

INDUSTRIAL FEATURES

Windmills

Oldest surviving Bourn, Cambridgeshire [East Anglia], a post mill built in 1636.

Oldest working Outwood near Redhill, Surrey [South East England], built in 1665.

Tallest traditional Sutton, Norfolk [East Anglia]. Built in 1853, the 9-storey tower carries sails 22.2 m [73 ft] in diameter.

Largest Burgar Hill, Orkney [Scottish Highlands and Islands]. First used on 10 November 1987, this electricity generating mill has a 37 m [121 ft] tall tower and 60 m [196 ft 10 in] blades generating 300 kW.

Tide mills

Oldest Woodbridge, Suffolk [East Anglia] has been the site of a tide mill continuously since the 12th century; the present mill was built in the 18th century.

Regular working Eling, Hampshire [Southern England] – the only tidal mill in the world producing flour on a regular basis.

Lighthouses

Most powerful Strumble Head near Fishguard [South Wales], where the beam strength has been recorded as 6 000 000 candelas.

Outwood Mill, Surrey.

Tallest Bishop Rock, Isles of Scilly [The South West], which stands 47.8 m [156.8 ft] high.

Remotest Sule Skerry [Scottish Highlands and Islands], 56 km [35 miles] offshore, 72 km [45 miles] north west of Dunnet Head.

Chimneys

Tallest Drax Power Station [Yorkshire and Humberside], topped out on 16 May 1969 – 259 m [850 ft] high and 26 m [85 ft] in diameter.

Cooling towers

Largest Ferrybridge [Yorkshire and Humberside] – 114 m [374 ft] high and 91 m [300 ft] wide at the base.

Towers

Tallest Emley Moor TV Tower [Yorkshire and Humberside]. Opened in September 1971, it weighs 15 000 tons and is 329.18 m [1080 ft] high.

Opposite: Bishop Rock Lighthouse.

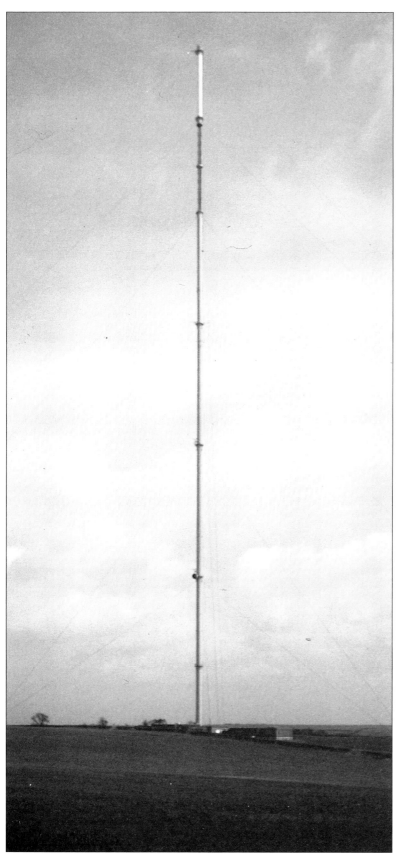

TV masts

Tallest Horncastle, Lincolnshire [East Midlands]. Built in 1965 and extended in 1967, it has a total height of 387.12 m [1272 ft].

Telephone exchanges

Busiest Beeston, Nottingham [East Midlands], which handles 1 558 000 calls per hour.

Transmissions line

Longest Severn Estuary [South Wales and West Country], where the support towers are each 148 m [488 ft] tall and the cable length is 1618 m [5310 ft].

Highest Thames Estuary [London and South East England], where the towers are each 192 m [630 ft] tall and the cables' minimum height above the Thames is 76 m [250 ft].

Barns

Longest Ipsden Barn, Oxfordshire [Thames and Chilterns], which is 117 m [385.5 ft] long and 9 m [30 ft] wide.

Below: Sherborne, Dorset, home of the longest tithe.

Longest tithe Wyke Farm, Sherborne Dorset [West Country] – 81 m [268 ft] long.

Left: Horncastle TV mast – the tallest in Britain.

The Strongbow Vat, Bulmers, Hereford.

Vats

argest Strongbow Vat, Bulmers, Her-
ord [Heart of England]. It measures
9.65 m [64.5 ft] high and 23 m [75.5 ft]
diameter and holds 74 099 hl
630 000 gallons] of cider.

Jetties

ongest Bee Ness Jetty near Rochester,
ent [South East England]. Completed
1930, it is 2500 m [8200 ft] long.

Breakwaters

Longest North Breakwater,
Holyhead, Anglesey [North
/ales], completed in 1873, 2394 m
.48 miles] long.

Stairs

ongest Cruachan Power Station [Scot-
sh Highlands and Islands], which has

1420 steps rising 324 m [1065 ft]; estimated climbing time is just under 30
minutes.

Escalators

Longest Tyne Tunnel [Northumbria].
Installed in 1951, it is 58.7 m [192 ft 8
in] long with a rise of 25.9 m [85 ft].

Travalators

Longest Terminal 3, Heathrow Airport
[London], which was installed in May
1970. It is 110.3 m [362 ft 2 in] long.

Lifts

Longest BBC TV Tower, West Moor
[Yorkshire and Humberside] – 283.4 m
[930 ft] long.

Gasholder

Largest No. 2 Holder, East Greenwich
Gas Works [London]. Built in 1891, it
measures 92 m [303 ft] in diameter and
is 45 m [148 ft] high with a capacity of
252 000 m^3 [8 900 000 cu. ft].

Hangers

Largest Britannia Assembly Hall, Filton
Airfield [West Country]. Completed in
September 1949, it covers an area of 3
ha [7½ acres] and is 321 m [1.054 ft]
wide.

Doors

Doors Britannia Assembly Hall, Filton
Airfield [West Country], which is 315
m [1035 ft] long and 20 m [67 ft] high,
divided into three equal sections.

Draglines

Largest Big Geordie, Butterwell [North-
umbria]. It weighs 3000 tons, has a

Holyhead, North Wales.

rward boom 48.7 m [160 ft] high, the
ain bucket is held on a boom 80.7 m
65 ft] long and has a capacity of 49.7
³ [65 cu. yards].

HEAVY INDUSTRY

Quarries

rgest Delabole Slate Quarry, Corn-
all [The West Country]. First
cavated in the 15th century, it has a
rcumference of 2.6 km [1.6 miles] and
depth of 150 m [500 ft].

ove: Delabole Slate Quarry.

Power stations

rgest Drax [Yorkshire and Humber-
le], fully operational from 1987
wards with six 660 MW generators
elding 3960 MW of power.

rst nuclear Calder Hall [Cumbria],
ened on 17 October 1956.

rgest hydroelectric Loch Sloy [South-
n Scotland] – its capacity is 130 MW.

pposite: Rhossili Bay, Gower
ninsula.

Wales

- **FIRST AREA OF OUTSTANDING NATURAL BEAUTY** – *The Gower Peninsular* – *1956*

- **FIRST STONE TOWER** – *Chepstow Castle* – AD1068

- **FIRST PURPOSE-BUILT CONCENTRIC CASTLE** – *Caerphilly Castle* – *1286*

- **THICKEST CASTLE WALLS** – *Flint Castle* – *7 m [23 ft] thick*

- **ONLY SURVIVING FORTIFIED BRIDGE** – *Monnow Bridge in Monmouth*

- **OLDEST STEAM RAILWAY STILL IN USE** – *Talyllyn Railway at Towyn* – *built in 1865*

- **LONGEST CABLE CAR** – *Llandudno Chairlift* – *1622 m [5320 ft]*

- **SMALLEST HOUSE** – *The Quay at Conwy*

- **ONLY WORKING RACK AND PINION RAILWAY** – *Snowdonia Mountain Railway*

The Llandudno chairlift.

Shipyards

Largest Harland and Wolff, Belfast [Northern Ireland], a 120 ha [300 acres] site including a 556 m [1825 ft] long and 93 m [305 ft] wide dry dock constructed in 1968–69 and capable a handling vessels up to 300 m [1000 ft] long and weighing 1 000 000 tons deadweight. The shipyard also contains Goliath and Sampson, the second and third largest fixed cranes in the world.

Oil refinery

Largest Fawley near Southampton, Hampshire [Southern England]. Opened in 1921 and expanded in 1951, it has a refining capacity of 15 600 000 tons of oil per year.

Gas works

Largest Breakwater Works, Plymouth [The West Country]. Opened in 1967, the site covers 7.6 ha [19 acres] and produces 1 415 850 m³ [50 000 000 cu. ft] of gas per day.

Brickworks

Largest London Brick Company, Stewartby, Bedfordshire [Thames and Chilterns]. Established in 1898, it is a 90 ha [221 acres] site producing an average of 10 500 000 bricks per week. It is the largest brickworks in the world.

Sewage works

Largest Beckton Works [London], which copes with a daily flow of 941 000 000 l [207 000 000 gallons] from a population of almost 3 000 000.

OFFICE AND FACTORY BUILDINGS

Largest Ford Parts Centre, Daventry, Northamptonshire [East Midlands], which opened on 6 September 1972. It measures 602 m [1975 ft] by 237 m [778

A fish display in the Harrods foodhall.

ft] on a 14.86 ha [36.7 acres] site and the building is fitted with 14 000 fluorescent lights.

Tallest Canary Tower, Canary Wharf, Docklands [London]. Designed by Caesar Pelli and opened in 1991, it has 50 storeys rising to height of 244 m [800 ft], making it the second tallest building in Europe.

Largest open-plan office British Gas West Midlands, Solihull, Warwickshire [Heart of England]. Opened in 1962, it measures 230 m [753 ft] by 49 m [160 ft] and holds 2125 staff.

Right: Canary Tower, Canary Wharf, London Docklands – Europe's second tallest building.

RETAIL OUTLETS

Shops

Largest shopping centre Gateshead MetroCentre [Northumbria]. Opened in October 1987 with shopping area of 145 000 m² [1 560 000 sq. ft] enclosing 340 shops, 35 stalls and 50 restaurants and cafes; it is the largest indoor shopping centre in Europe.

Longest shopping mall Milton Keynes [Thames and Chilterns], measuring 650 m [2133 ft] long it is the longest in the world.

Largest department store Harrods, Knightsbridge [London]. Founded as a grocery shop by Henry Charles Harrod in 1849, it now employs between 4000 and 5000 staff to cover 200 departments with 9 ha [22 acres] of selling space. The record annual turnover is £312 000 000, while the record one-day turnover is £7 000 000.

Largest menswear shop Slater Menswear, Glasgow [Glasgow], where the sales area is 3740 m² [40 250 sq. ft], carrying a stock of 17 000 suits with weekly sales averaging 2000 suits. It is the largest in the world.

Largest toyshop Hamley's, Regent's Street [London]. Founded in 1760, it has 4180 m² [45 000 sq. ft] of selling space, making it the largest in the world.

Largest bookshop Foyles, Charing Cross Road [London], founded in 1906. The five-storey building displays approximately 6 000 000 books on 48 km [30 miles] of shelving. In terms of stock carried, it is the largest bookshop in the world.

Largest record shop The HMV Shop, Oxford Street [London]. Opened on 24 October 1986, it has 3408 m² [36 684 sq. ft] of selling space and is the largest in the world.

Largest photographic shop Jessop of Leicester Photo Centre, Leicester [East Midlands]. Opened in June 1979, the sales area is 2508 m² [27 000 sq. ft].

Post offices

Oldest Sanquhar [Southern Scotland], which was established in 1763 – before the creation of the Royal Mail – to serve a horse-ridden service to Edinburgh.

Largest George Square [Glasgow], where the counter is 47.8 m [157 ft] long with 22 serving positions.

Oldest pillar box Barnes Cross, Holwell, Dorset [West Country], 1853.

Gateshead MetroCentre, Northumbria.

Breathtaking Lulworth Cove is part of the Dorset coastline.

INDEX

Lough Neagh, Co. Antrim.

People Index